Efficiency and Effort

Efficiency and Effort

AN ANALYSIS OF
INDUSTRIAL ADMINISTRATION

W. BALDAMUS

TAVISTOCK PUBLICATIONS

First published in 1961
by Tavistock Publications (1959) Limited
11 New Fetter Lane, London, E.C.4
and printed in Great Britain
in 11/12 pt. Times New Roman
by the Alcuin Press
Welwyn Garden City

To Eva and Derrick Pritchatt

CONTENTS

ACKNOWLEDGEMENTS

THE preparations for this study reach back over many years during the course of which I have been influenced by other scholars in a general way that could not be expressed adequately in the text. I had the benefit of unfailing help and constructive criticism, especially on methodological questions, from Christian von Ferber. I am also deeply indebted to Adolphe Lowe for his many contributions to the fundamental problems of the sociological premises of economics. More specifically, the psychological discussion in Part II owes much to the patient criticism of Derrick Pritchatt. Being a strict behaviourist, his task was all the more difficult, as I am in this field an amateur with an 'introspective' bias. Finally, a constant source of inspiration has been Thomas A. Ryan's pioneer work on the concept of effort in industrial psychology.

W. B.

Introduction

THIS study is concerned with fundamental aspects of industrial organization that have been neglected in the past. Its purpose is to show that the organization of industry, with all its complexities and diversities, ultimately revolves on a single process: the administrative process through which the employee's effort is controlled by the employer. This means that the entire system of industrial production will be viewed as a system of administrative controls which regulate quantity, quality, and distribution of human effort.

The problem has received surprisingly little attention within the conventional framework of current theory and research. The reason is this. It has been customary to describe the organization of industrial and business activities in terms of efficiency, not effort. Concepts such as efficient management, efficient labour, and efficiency of administration are, at present, the keynote of both popular and academic discussions on industrial affairs. But what *is* efficiency? Despite its obvious importance, the question is rarely asked. It is generally assumed that no formal definition is required because the meaning of the word is firmly established on a common-sense basis.[1] According to common sense, an organization's or a person's behaviour is judged as efficient or inefficient by comparing input and output in terms of some unit, chosen arbitrarily, such as money, effort, physical resources, etc. It is characteristic of the common-sense notion that the nature of the unit does not seem to require a precise and formal definition. There is usually no need to mention the unit at all.

[1] There are, for example, textbooks in which the concept of 'efficiency' is of crucial importance though it remains undefined; cf. H. Simon (1946). For a more sophisticated attempt to avoid a formal definition cp. J. M. Keynes (1936) pp. 135ff, 231ff, 307ff.

(All references in this study are reduced to the name of the author and year of publication; the full title is contained in the list of references on p. 129).

1

Introduction

Though it may well be sufficient to rely on common sense for day-to-day administrative practice, its use in scientific inquiry is a different matter. Here it means that the familiarity and simplicity of such words is deceptive. It creates a sense of certainty for which there is no justification. As a result many empirical investigations on industrial organization are, scientifically, of questionable significance. The convenient custom of taking the criteria, and therefore the meaning, of efficiency for granted has created the impression that systematic theoretical work is dispensable, and common sense, not theory, is at present the main source from which research hypotheses in this field are obtained.

But this is not just a matter of language. By using familiar, yet undefined, words, a host of value judgements unnoticeably attached to them is also taken over. As the word 'efficiency' has no scientific fundament, we are inclined to assume without question that to maximize efficiency is desirable if not indeed the chief purpose of industrial enterprise. We believe as a matter of course, and on the strength of an unassailable tradition, that efficient conduct is preferable to inefficiency. It is similarly assumed, without explicit justification, that efficiency is inseparably associated with 'productivity', which is an equally valued and desirable goal. Thus strikes, restriction of output, or other forms of unproductive behaviour are never described as efficient, however carefully organized and effective they may be from the standpoint of the wage-earner. An 'efficient strike would seem to be a contradiction in terms, even when it is part of a perfectly rational strategy in the course of wage bargaining.

However, the concealed intrusion of conventional prejudices goes further than that. Inductive studies on industrial problems are rarely conceived in common-sense terms alone. Quite frequently they include some reference to theoretical concepts as well, so that it is the *mixture* of common sense and technical analysis that presents the real difficulty, a mixture by no means easily sorted out. This is best illustrated by the application of technical economics to problems of industrial organization. The custom here is to combine general criteria of economic

2

analysis with inductive observations, mostly concerned with efficiency, which are taken from business records or official industrial statistics. It is often thought that empirical (including statistical) generalizations obtained from such sources and expressed in those terms are relevant to economics in order to test the validity of theoretical propositions.

Unfortunately, this is an illusion. Though the actual words used in economics and industrial practice are often the same, their meaning is not. The scientific foundation of modern economic analysis rests on the principle that economic behaviour is determined solely by *subjective* choice or preference of an individual concerning the alternative usefulness of relatively scarce means.[1] But in the real world of industrial organization we find the very opposite. Here we have essentially technological conceptions, derived from objective properties and magnitudes: physical products, energy consumption, numbers employed, amounts of effort, hours of work, and so on. So we have a very paradoxical situation. The modern trend towards an increasingly formalized general-equilibrium theory has been a continuous process whereby subjective and relativistic criteria have replaced the remnants of the classical school which was focused on the objective physical substance of material welfare, notably 'real costs' in the form of labour resources; and yet as far as the practice of industrial administration is concerned, objective physical conceptions have not only survived, but are the very soul of it. This is most clearly indicated by the importance which businessmen and administrators attach to efficiency as a decisive attribute of the firm's, the management's, and the worker's behaviour; for in all this efficiency does not involve a subjective choice among competing ends; it is tacitly, though quite generally, understood in the sense of 'economizing' with the physical and human sources of material welfare, that is to say: in terms of real costs.

In one branch of applied economics this confusion of common sense and technical terms has finally produced insuperable difficulties. Industrial administration is in many ways concerned

[1] See for example L. Robbins (1937); J. Stigler (1947).

3

with industrial relations and the study of this has been traditionally conceived (by economists) as a problem of wage determination and wage bargaining, which means a problem to which the marginal-productivity theory of wages seemed applicable. But more and more it has been recognized that the really decisive factors in wage determination revolve on matters that are quite remote from the theoretical model of an employer who chooses among alternative uses of relatively scarce resources of labour. The decisive elements are, again, real costs in the physical sense and not opportunity costs. Real costs are in practice associated with variations in labour efficiency, which in turn are interpreted as differences in the wage-earner's 'effort'. More particularly, it is the conception of 'normal' or 'required' effort on which wage administration is based. Obviously, such notions have no place in existing theory. The difficulty has been aggravated by the fact that the normal level of effort is not simply an independent variable that could be taken as given, but is itself controlled by a large number of administrative and institutional factors in the formal organization of industrial enterprise: methods of production, size of plant, methods of payment and promotion, employee recruitment, and so on. Since all this is outside the realm of economic analysis, the control of effort is as much beyond the scope of applied economics as the study of industrial efficiency in general. It is not surprising, therefore, that a great deal of currently applied economics amounts merely to a description, not an explanation, of the expectations and conceptions that are characteristic of the common-sense framework of the business world. Though frequently overlooked by economists, this fact is well recognized among those who have extensive experience of business administration. To quote Chester Barnard, the foremost authority on this matter: 'I am asked to state to what extent and how economic facts and general economic knowledge govern my decisions in an organization. It is only with difficulty that I comprehend the question. It relates to a kind of world of which I have no experience—an economic world' (Barnard, 1938, p. 239).

4

What appears to be necessary, therefore, is an investigation of the physical, non-economic aspects of efficiency, those which matter in real life and which are not amenable to economic analysis. Taken in the broadest sense, they comprise two types of factor: technological and human resources. We shall confine ourselves to the latter, that is to say, we shall be concerned with 'labour efficiency' the physical substance of which is human effort. The reason for selecting the human factor in efficiency lies in the fact that it alone is relevant to social science. What we are proposing, then, is that the social problems of efficiency are ultimately problems of the control of human effort. Thus the larger and more intangible question of overall efficiency can be narrowed down to the more specific problem of defining and analysing the meaning of effort. For 'effort', again, is merely a common-sense term that is scientifically useless. In pursuing this question, we shall, in fact, find that it is surprisingly difficult to determine the substance of effort. Though the particular definition we shall suggest must, to some extent, remain tentative, the problem can no longer be avoided. Unless *some* concept of effort is analytically established, the student of industrial organization will have to admit that the essence of his subject-matter is unknown.

Since economic analysis is irrelevant in this field, one might expect sociology to have filled the gap. But this is only true in a very limited sense. There is as yet no specifically sociological theory of industrial organization. What is usually called 'industrial sociology' consists basically of empirical investigations, loosely organized around a few general concepts. Most familiar among these is the distinction between formal and informal organization, an idea which has by now achieved all the assurance of textbook status.[1] The distinction more or less retains the form in which it first took shape in Durkheim's contractual versus noncontractual elements of social order.[2] According to

[1] Cp. the two most represenative textbooks of industrial sociology: Wilbert E. Moore (2nd ed. 1951) and D. C. Miller and W. B. Form (1951).
[2] Cf. *The Division of Labour in Society*; translated by G. Simpson (1947), chap. VIII, pp. 200ff.

5

that theory, the noncontractual cohesion of the social order is *prior* (and not merely supplementary) to any formal relations organized by contracts. Thus, in order to adapt the theory to the special sphere of industrial organization, it would have been necessary to construct a precise connection between the informal and formal order in that context. But no special theory of this kind has ever been formulated. Nor did Elton Mayo and his followers have any success when they tried to demonstrate empirically that informal social relations among employees determine the shape of formal organization. There is no conclusive evidence, for example, that a higher level of employee morale results in greater efficiency. Today we know that the belief in the supremacy of 'human relations' over formal organization lives on only in popular misconceptions that have come to surround these attempts, and from which, no doubt, they often drew their inspiration.

Most disappointing has been the failure of sociology to penetrate those problems of industrial administration which have remained unsolved (or neglected) within the conventional approach of applied economics: the problems of labour efficiency and effort control. This failure is explained partly by the erroneous supposition that these matters are already taken care of in economics. Another reason is that industrial sociologists and applied economists share an important postulate that makes it difficult for either to go beyond common-sense interpretations. That postulate is the assumption that the organization of industry as a whole reveals a natural harmony of interests between employers and employees. There are many versions of this; both economic and sociological inquiries are committed, for instance, to the belief that efficiency is equally beneficial to management and workers. Furthermore, a common point of departure is to interpret industrial disorganization as a superficial and temporary imperfection in a system that fundamentally maintains an autonomous equilibrium between sectional interests; on this basis strikes, restriction of output, absenteeism, and other symptoms of disorganization are merely the result of inadequate communication between

6

employers and employees, or due to unavoidable misunderstandings or irresponsible conduct. Another aspect of this is the idea that there is, at least in the long run, occupational mobility up and down the status hierarchy: wage-earners will become employers (or managers) and employers will hire themselves out as wage-earners, whenever—temporarily—the distribution of earned income (and other rewards) in relation to effort (and similar sacrifices) is unequal. It is evidently this particular type of assumed 'substitutability' of different roles which ultimately guarantees a pre-established and lasting harmony of interests.

The main advantage of this theoretical postulate is that it projects some order into the complex system of industrial affairs as far as its smooth and orderly working goes. However, the deeper institutional forces that promote an effective co-operation between employer and employees are assumed as given; and, being unproblematical, they are never explained. A still more serious defect lies in the existence of the numerous manifestations of conflict and disorganization. Since they are supposed to be due merely to misunderstandings, it becomes very difficult to explain why they are in fact a permanent feature of the present scene. As more and more observations have accumulated, the apparent consistency in the pattern of industrial unrest has become increasingly perplexing, just as the assumption of a basic harmony of interests has made it difficult to comprehend the functions of trade unionism and collective bargaining as part of the institutional framework of industrial society.

The present study attempts a different approach. We shall assume from the start that employer-employee relations present a structure of differentiated power that reflects unequally distributed advantages and disadvantages. Consequently the emphasis will be on the causes of conflict and disorganization. This will have the advantage of obtaining a more consistent explanation of the relevant observations than has so far been possible. But some unexpected difficulties will also arise. Once the assumption of a harmonious and self-regulating system is removed, we are faced with the vastly complicated jungle of

B

industrial administration that would seem to be without any system at all. If conflict is basic and unavoidable, how do we account for the apparent stability of employer-employee relations when there are no strikes, no grievances, no dissatisfactions? In other words, it is now the ordinary pursuit of work, the daily run of routine activities, that has to be explained.

The obvious way of dealing with new questions of a complex nature would be to construct a simplified model with new assumptions and concepts. The assumptions should be stated explicitly and the technical terms should avoid the pernicious influence of common-sense words and conventional phrases. The need for such a carefully constructed theory of industrial organization has been increasingly recognized, and there have been a few attempts in that direction. But nobody seems to realize that the scope for such innovations is severely limited. This stems from a single but formidable fact: the large and ever-growing accumulation of empirical observations in the field. It might be argued that much of this material could be ignored because its validity is uncertain. Such an attitude would seem to be justified on the ground that at present most investigations, however extensive and elaborate, simply produce detailed repetitions of established facts. But this is not altogether true, for now and then there are *unexpected* results. These accidental observations neither confirm nor contradict preconceived notions, but appear to assert themselves just because they are inexplicable in relation to established assumptions. Though it is difficult to prove, it is at least feasible that such observations form a potentially significant contribution towards a more penetrating interpretation. They certainly cannot be ignored.

Thus a radically novel framework of concepts would be useless. The desirable degree of precision must at present be sacrificed in order that observations available only in non-technical terms, but nevertheless potentially relevant, may be utilized. This study is therefore based on a moderate level of abstraction that permits a reasonably close contact with the data of past research. There will be only a small number of new concepts and even these are not the result of rigorous theorizing, but rather of a process of unending trial and error which took shape during the process of empirical work.[1] The unfamiliarity of these concepts will make a difficult and seemingly unrealistic presentation unavoidable, quite apart from the fact that our subject-matter is unusually complicated. To facilitate the subsequent discussion, the main simplifying abstractions may be stated in advance. They are two in number.

1. A constant source of confusion has been the word 'human relations'. Its vagueness conceals the important difference between two types of relationship: *employer-employee relations* on the one hand and *employee relations* on the other. The latter concerns the interactions (both formal and informal) between people of similar status and occupation. These we shall deliberately neglect by arguing that the crucial and unsolved problems of industrial organization and disorganization are connected only with employer-employee relations. Friendships and hostilities among employees themselves are only indirectly relevant, in so far as they may be a response to particular aspects of industrial conflict.

2. A further simplification will be introduced by separating two institutions that are in the real world closely interlocked: '*occupation*' and 'employment'. The significance of this distinction will only gradually emerge in the course of the analysis. For the moment a rough approximation will do. Both institutions are to a large extent regulated by one and the same mechanism, namely, through the market process by which a given activity is compensated through the payment of wages, salaries, and other rewards. The difference is that these compensations are determined in different ways. 'Occupation' requires that 'occupational costs' connected with the acquisition of skill, experience, and occupational education are compensated.

[1] Conceptual improvisation on the basis of trial and error seems as yet the only way of coping with the difficulties of scientific method in this context. The more profound limitations of theoretical work have been persistently—and often grossly—underestimated by empirical investigators. For the most incisive study of this problem cp. N. Elias (1956), especially pp. 238ff.

9

Introduction

Such costs are reflected, for instance, in that component of the wage structure which expresses skill differentials. As to 'employment', the decisive criterion is the compensation for 'effort'. Though often concealed, it appears perhaps most clearly in such differentials as derive from the difference in average effort between daywork and piecework. It will be shown that variations in effort (and the corresponding rewards) are as much a *universal* component of industrial organization as the more obvious diversification of occupations. (This is a statement of fact which should be taken on trust for the time being.) Now, in order to isolate the strategic aspects of industrial organization (and disorganization), we shall argue that it is employment—and effort—rather than occupation which is essentially problematical. So we shall concentrate on the institution of employment, neglecting the corresponding aspects of occupation. However, the empirical justification for this procedure is far from obvious. It has to be shown that the whole range of efficient administration, including methods of production, renumeration, and supervision is centred on the control of effort and not on occupational costs. The analytical process of separating the two components of industrial organization presents the key to a number of unexplored problems. Above all it will explain the curious mixture of stability and instability, of peaceful co-operation and permanent strife that is characteristic of advanced industrial society. For everything that points to a 'harmony' of interests appears to be connected with the self-regulating mechanism of occupational costs and rewards within the institution of occupation. And the causes of recurrent disorganization stem from an unbalanced and variable distribution of effort and effort rewards in the context of employment. The significance of this contrast can be seen at a glance from the fact that occupational costs are strictly determinate whereas effort is not. Effort is neither measurable nor easily defined in terms of any tangible criteria.

The combined result of the two methods of analytical simplification amounts to this. Our task will be narrowly confined to employer-employee relations within the institution of employment (which is centred on the control of effort). It should, however, not be overlooked that the difference between 'horizontal' employee relations and 'vertical' employer-employee relations corresponds to the more general distinction between role and status, a distinction that is also applicable to the institution of occupation. How the focus of our analysis is located in this larger area of industrial sociology may be visualized from the scheme shown below. It will, moreover, be evident from this arrangement that the usual practice of using the concepts 'role' and 'status' more or less interchangeably is grossly misleading: it invites the almost universally accepted fallacy that the difference between being an employer and an employee is one of role content rather than status.[1]

Role Relations ('horizontal')	*Occupation* Occupational Role Structure	*Employment* Employee Relations
Status Relations ('vertical')	Interaction between different ranks of Occupational Hierarchy	Employer-Employee Relations

For the rest, the familiar theorem of formal versus informal relations will be used, with certain modifications. This frame of reference will not seem so vague when we realize that it is applicable to each of the four aspects mentioned above, though we shall be using it only in its application to employment relations between employer and employee. We shall also develop a further device to make the conventional approach more rigorous. This is a distinction, with respect to the informal (non-contractual) order, between the general framework of 'social supports' and specific 'institutional controls'; the former being the product of primary, and the latter of secondary processes

[1] Cf. for example Eugene V. Schneider (1957), pp. 11ff and passim.

11

of socialization. Of course, the particular content of these factors varies according to whether we are dealing with occupation or employment, employee relations or employer-employee relations; here we shall focus on the institutionalized expectations underlying the control of effort. The resulting frame of

Formal Relations between Employer and Employee	**Administrative Effort Controls** (Methods of Production, Wage Payment, etc.) concerning: Effort Stability Effort Intensity

↑

| *Informal Relations* between Employer and Employee { | *Institutional Controls* (Secondary Socialization) | Standardized Effort Values   Wage Disparity Norms |
| | *Social Supports* (Primary Socialization) | ↑

Work Obligations |

reference (in which the main causal connections are indicated by arrows) is as shown in the Schema opposite:

The attempt to trace back through a number of interrelated factors to a comparatively simple complex of social forces will make it necessary for us to re-examine the conventional treatment of these problems in order to disclose unexplained residuals and inconsistencies that do not make sense within the framework of the traditional assumptions. First we shall demonstrate the unique importance of administrative effort controls to industrial efficiency (Part I). For that the common-sense meaning of 'effort' will be sufficient. But further inquiry will make necessary a more detailed analysis of the components and manifestations of effort (Part II). Finally (in Part III) the problem of the institutional and social environment of effort controls will be taken up. Here it will be seen that the social foundations of industrial activity do not merely support their formal organization in a remote and indirect manner that may be taken for granted. The decisive point is that the effective control over the means of industrial administration is directly and solely a function of specific institutionalized expectations; ultimately they determine the relative shares of the proceeds of industry between employers and employee.

PART I

Industrial Administration

CHAPTER 1

Ineffective Controls

THERE are many ways in which social and institutional forces affect the system of contractual (formal) relations between employers and employees. Some may be identified as causal determinants, others have only a vaguely diffused conditioning effect. In between these extremes are those which are most characteristic of the industrial sphere: factors setting a *limiting margin* within which a given formal control operates effectively. As a rule we shall be concerned only with this latter type of marginal conditions. Even here there are differences. Certain conditions are immediately obvious, whereas others seem to be concealed by intervening factors. For example, if we take employee supervision as a method of formal control, it is evident that it can function adequately only if the employees have a minimal cooperative attitude towards the supervisor. The existence of particular social or institutional conditions limiting the controlling function of the labour market is, on the other hand, less apparent; that wage determination and wage policy are completely dependent on social forces has only very recently been discovered.[1]

This is a province where, for a long time, a highly formalized system of economic analysis has been available in the theory of wages. However, economic analysis has nothing to do with the organization of industrial effort, efficiency, and productivity; its objective is to analyse only the *effects* of the interaction of these forces—their effects, that is to say, in terms of market values. It is true that on any level of abstraction lower than that of pure theory, observations about industrial organization and administration enter in many ways into the economist's field of vision; he is concerned, for example, with factors of human

[1] See notably Barbara Wootton (1955); F. Fürstenberg (1958).

choices and decisions that partly determine the processes of wage settlement, risk-taking, or investment. But in all this the dominant aim is always to translate these forces as conveniently as possible into factors of supply and demand that are amenable to the basic rules of equilibrium analysis. This, it should be noticed, is always possible, however varied and complex the original data on motives and decisions may be. In the present context, perhaps the best illustration of the surprisingly wide scope of this method is Hicks' Theory of Wages (1932). The kind of analysis that will follow here is not only different, but diametrically opposed. Instead of trying to reduce any 'peculiarity' in the behaviour of wage-earners and employers, arising from special social, psychological, or technological conditions, to the terms of market behaviour, we shall do the opposite by starting with certain *defects* in the system of regulative controls, defects that cannot be dismissed as human 'imperfections' because they have a logic of their own that must, ultimately, be traced back to the social and institutional foundations of the system itself.

How do we discover defects of this kind? Since the purpose of formal controls is to achieve a stable organization of economic activities, the defects would have to be cases of permanent or continuously recurrent *instability*. Under present conditions we seem confronted with nothing more serious than a mild form of industrial 'unrest', a vague and varying phenomenon, somehow connected with inflationary trends in wages, profits, and prices, and with certain types of strike, absenteeism, the employment of foreign labour, and so on. Such unrest is not generally understood as being symptomatic of a permanent instability in the system of formal controls.

There was, however, a period immediately after the War, when a few of these symptoms were of a more serious nature. With the advent of institutionalized full employment, absenteeism and labour turnover in many industries became excessively high and were combined with what was then called a general decline in labour 'discipline'. As it was widely admitted by employers and industrial leaders that the problem was insoluble

18

—short of reducing the level of employment—this form of industrial disorganization was obviously a case of fundamental instability and not just a matter of superficial 'unrest'. If the problem receives less attention today, it does not mean that it has been solved within the scope of available controls. What has partly happened is that management has resigned itself to a condition where, in certain occupations, there is always an unstable labour force. Partly also, the introduction of foreign labour into some of these occupations has temporarily made the problem less conspicuous.

We must therefore inquire more closely into the question of labour instability on the basis of relevant facts.[1] Let us take labour turnover first. No information is available that would show conclusively that there is an inverse relation between level of unemployment and rates of labour turnover. But we have some evidence that suggests such a relationship within certain limits. In comparing unemployment figures for July 1951 and July 1952, from data published in the *Ministry of Labour Gazette*, it appears that there was an increase, particularly in the Midland Region where unemployment among both men and women more than doubled. If these figures are set against labour turnover records taken from a firm employing approximately 16,000 workers in different factories both in the Midlands and elsewhere, it will be seen that labour turnover decreased markedly among men and women not only in the Midlands but also in the 'Other Regions' (*Table 1*).

Although, as a matter of common sense, it would not seem surprising that full employment leads to 'over-mobility' of labour, it is not easily explained in terms of formal controls. One can only say, negatively, that wages or wage differentials have nothing to do with it. Of course, there must always be a minimum of labour turnover if wage movements are to be effective

[1] I refer to an extensive investigation of labour turnover and absence, chiefly in the Midlands, conducted by the Faculty of Commerce of the University of Birmingham. The information quoted in the following is merely intended to illustrate the problem. For further data and for all technical details see W. Baldamus and H. Behrend (1950); Baldamus (1951b); J. Long (1951); Behrend (1951); Behrend (1953).

TABLE 1   COMPARISON OF UNEMPLOYMENT AND LABOUR
TURNOVER IN 1951 AND 1952*

	1951	1952
UNEMPLOYMENT		
Percentage Rates in Mid-July		
Midland Region		
Men	·3	·7
Women	·4	1·3
Great Britain		
Men	·9	1·5
Women	·9	2·6
LABOUR TURNOVER		
Half-Annual Percentage Rates for different		
factories of one company		
Midlands		
Men	39	25
Women	53	38
Other Regions		
Men	30	15
Women	38	26

* H. Behrend (1953), pp. 69 and 77.

in producing required shifts in the distribution of labour among different jobs, areas, and industries. Those firms from which workers move away will show an increase in labour turnover rates, for the rates measure the number of leavers as a percentage of the number employed. It is difficult to say what this minimum should be. On the basis of practical experience it is certain that if substantially more than a quarter of the employees leave within a year (that is to say, annual turnover rates are over 25 per cent), labour turnover is excessive. The figures in *Table 1* for 1951, and even for 1952, are clearly of that order (they have to be doubled to give annual rates). In that case there are workers who float between different firms without ever settling down. This kind of over-mobility cannot possibly be a function of the labour market. Other factors must be at work.

This becomes evident when labour turnover data is broken down according to occupational stratification within a given company or department. It appears then that under full employment remarkable differences in turnover rates for different types of jobs and occupations can be found (Baldamus (1951b), pp.

44ff.). If in some occupations workers are always unstable and in others not, the inescapable conclusion is that a specific *occupational* factor is responsible. *Table 2*, which may serve as an illustration, suggests that this factor is connected to some extent with differences in the level of skill and the length of the work cycle: the lower the skill and the more repetitive the type of work, the higher the rate of labour turnover.

Another indication of occupational factors is the curious phenomenon that rates of absence tend to show a stable pattern if analysed in terms of day-to-day changes during the week. For example, in companies working a five-day week, the number of absentees is highest on Monday, decreasing steadily each day to a minimum on Friday. This is shown in *Table 3*. It can also be seen that if the annual average level of total absence rates declines from year to year, as was the case between 1946 and 1950, the deviation between average Monday and Friday absenteeism decreases accordingly. Surely, these phenomena cannot possibly be accounted for by wage inequities. As a matter of fact, it appears that the deviation between Monday and Friday absence decreases as the level of skill increases.[1] In the case of highly skilled tool-makers and floor-moulders, for example, the decrease of absenteeism during the week was barely noticeable; with unskilled workers it was as much as 50 per cent; semi-skilled workers were about half way between these extremes. Moreover, when this investigation was extended to grammar school teachers, it was found that absence *increased* from Monday to Friday.

These effects of type of work on labour turnover and absence can be fully understood only after a closer study of the motivation to work. For the moment, however, they are sufficiently instructive to show that full employment in an inflationary

---

[1] Baldamus and Behrend (1950); Behrend (1951). It should be noted, generally, that the effect of type of work on absence must be taken into account, particularly when the relation between size of firm and level of absence is examined; since the relative number of skilled workers decreases with increasing size of firm, this may well explain why the level of absence increases with size of firm. This has been overlooked in a study by the Acton Society Trust (1953), which otherwise confirms the decline of absence during the week.

economy creates instability of labour chiefly at the lower levels of skill and particularly with regard to monotonous or unpleasant work. If either some degree of unemployment or, alternatively, the use of foreign labour is necessary to make these marginal occupations stable, that would amount to a measure of *coercive* pressure that is not normally implied by the available system of formal controls, such as the labour market, methods of promotion, wage incentives, and so on. The current interpretation of these controls supposes them to be based on voluntary contractual relations. The emergence of marginal occupations where labour is inherently unstable proves that this framework of controls is partially ineffective. It is immaterial that our

TABLE 2   ANNUAL LABOUR TURNOVER RATES, LENGTH OF TRAINING, AND WORK-CYCLE FOR DIFFERENT TYPES OF WORK IN ONE COMPANY*†

Type of Work	Av. No. Employed	T.O. Rates %	Training Period	Approx. Work Cycle
Enamellers	23	96	2 weeks	1–5 mins.
Heavy servicers	120	89	None	Varying
Crane drivers	46	68	2 months	5 mins.
Packers	43	53	2 weeks	30 mins.
Capstan Operators	113	40	2 months	2–15 mins.
Light servicers	247	36	None	5 mins.
Store assemblers	115	31	3 months	30 mins–8 hrs.
Press-operators	47	26	2 months	10–30 secs.
Millers	50	26	Up to 1 month	30 mins.
Drillers	122	26	Up to 1 month	5–15 mins.
Painters	49	25	3 months	5 mins.
Testers	72	24	3 months–5 yrs.	1–5 hrs.
Inspectors	67	21	12 months	5–30 mins.
Assemblers	350	20	3–6 months	5 mins.
Welders (electric and gas)	60	20	3–6 months	10–30 mins.
Turners (production)	31	19	1–3 months	10 mins.
Corebuilders	61	13	6 months	1–3 hrs.
Winders (electric motors)	126	11	6 months –2 yrs.	3–14 days
Fitters	199	7	5 yrs.	1–8 weeks
Toolsetters	113	6	2 yrs.	1 hr.
Toolmakers	104	4	5 yrs.	1–8 weeks
Patternmakers	53	4	5 yrs.	1–12 weeks
Floor moulders	68	3	5 yrs.	2–5 days

* Source: W. Baldamus (1951), p. 52.
† Annual T.O. Rates for 1949, women excluded.

observations are limited to particular aspects of instability; there may well be many other indications of a similar kind. The relevant point is that the observed type of ineffective organization is clearly of strategic importance to the whole system of formal controls.

TABLE 3   AVERAGE DAILY ABSENCE RATES FOR 1946–1950 AT ONE COMPANY*

	1946		1947 6-day week (7 weeks)		1947 5-day week Mar.–Dec.		1948		1949		1950	
	Absence Rate %	Difference from Friday's Absence Rate	Absence Rate %	Difference from Friday's Absence Rate	Absence Rate %	Difference from Friday's Absence Rate	Absence Rate %	Difference from Friday's Absence Rate	Absence Rate %	Difference from Friday's Absence Rate	Absence Rate %	Difference from Friday's Absence Rate
Saturday	16·1	6·9	11·8	1·9	–	–	–	–	–	–	–	–
Monday	10·9	1·7	11·6	1·7	8·8	1·6	7·5	1·5	7·1	1·4	6·5	1·2
Tuesday	10·4	1·2	10·8	·9	8·3	1·1	7·1	1·1	6·8	1·1	6·3	1·0
Wednesday	10·2	1·0	11·0	1·1	8·0	·8	7·0	1·0	6·4	·7	5·9	·6
Thursday	9·8	·6	10·5	·6	7·7	·5	6·6	·6	6·2	·5	5·7	·4
Friday	9·2	–	9·9	–	7·2	–	6·0	–	5·7	–	5·3	–
Total Deviation from Friday / Average Absence Rate	11·1	11·4	10·4	6·2†	8·0	4·0	6·9	4·2	6·5	3·7	5·9	3·2

* Average number employed: 7,000 workers. The figures are based on full working weeks. Holiday periods have been excluded when calculating the average.
  † Excluding Saturday, the total deviation is 4·5 for 1946 and 4·3 for 1947.

CHAPTER 2

Occupational Controls

IT is difficult to determine why the system is ineffective. As we are concerned with the system as a whole, a factor of general significance must be responsible. Looking at the problem as broadly as possible, we shall find that there are two different types of industrial control that appear to operate side by side: occupational controls and effort controls. They will be discussed, in that order, in this and the following two chapters.

The term 'occupational controls' refers to *earned incomes* in so far as they control the number of people in different occupations through changes in supply and demand. It might seem that the term 'labour market' has the same meaning. However, this is a concept that tends to be associated with wage-earners only. By contrast, occupational controls should be taken widely enough to cover *any* kind of earned income and corresponding occupation, including particularly the salaries of managers. We can, if necessary, go further than that. Economists have repeatedly tried to identify the entrepreneur's services by pointing to some special function that he has to fulfil, such as 'co-ordinating' the factors of production, or 'innovating' new methods of production. Profits are, from this point of view, merely a special kind of earned income.[1] Theoretically, therefore, there is no need to discriminate between entrepreneurs and managerial personnel. Industrial disputes are generally understood as a conflict between 'labour' and 'management' in the widest sense, and this will suffice for the following analysis.

---

[1] Joseph Schumpeter's theory of profits, derived from a specific concept of innovation, offers many advantages from the sociological point of view. Cp. A. Lowe (1935), pp. 83–91; A. Lowe (1951); T. Parsons and N. J. Smelser (1956), pp. 26, 65f, 266.

24

The substitution of 'occupational controls' for the conventional term 'labour market' is not just a matter of convenient terminology, but has important conseqeunces. It will reveal that two seemingly different problems, unconnected in the past, are really two aspects of the same problem. There is, on the one hand, the question of wage differentials, which refers solely to income relations between different sections of employees. On the other hand, we have the problem of income relations between employers and employees. On the face of it, the two issues would seem incomparable and it is of course obvious that the social and political conflicts that surround them are very different. If, however, the employer's earned income is just as much a reward for occupational services as are wages, logically we are dealing with the same problem. In each case we are confronted with (earned) income differentials that are dependent on the functions of the market mechanism, and in each case the crucial question is how this mechanism, as a form of regulative control, determines the structure of differentials. Since all methods of production, and thus all products that are marketed, require a combination of different occupational services, the problem is ultimately one of imputation: to interpret the rewards for these services as differential shares in the product.

The shares of different sections of employees in the product—wage-differentials—appear to be less intangible than the shares between employers and employees. Struggles over wage-differentials have become so dominant a factor in the contemporary scene of industrial organization that they tend to overshadow everything else, for indeed they do cover a wide area of industrial relations. They impinge upon the conflicting economic interests of workers in different occupations, industries, localities, types of work; between men and women; and they include age, skill, and status differentials.[1] It is therefore not surprising that current wage policy is centred on wage differentials. This can easily be seen for example, from Barbara Wootton's recent analysis in *The Social Foundations of Wage Policy* (B. Wootton

[1] For a comprehensive and well-informed evaluation of the whole problem area cp. F. Fürstenberg (1958).

(1955), chaps. IV and V). There are three major arguments for wage (and salary) demands:

1. Changes in the cost of living.
2. Undermanning of particular industries, trades, or skills.
3. The need to maintain the existing wage-structure.

While the latter two arguments are directly related to the dynamic and the static aspects, respectively, of wage differentials, the cost-of-living issue has a similar effect indirectly. The rising cost of living is not usually invoked to back up claims for a general rise of all earned incomes, but chiefly to defend the wage claim of a *particular* section of workers, or a trade union or profession. Thus, the problem of wage-differentials presents the widest aspect of industrial conflict at the present time.

Any attempt to analyse the renumeration for different kinds of labour is bound to come up against the fact that they are intractably *combine*d in making a given product (just as capital is combined with labour). The one and only source for all occupational rewards is the market price of some product or group of products. Neither economic theory nor common sense provides a simple and sufficiently general answer as to how the relative shares of these contributions to the product are determined, e.g., why different amounts of wages go to skilled and unskilled work, to manual and non-manual effort, to direct and indirect labour. This makes it understandable that the imputation of wages to different kinds of labour is open to ethical judgements in the same way as the struggle over profits and wages: all the popular arguments over wage-differentials can always be reduced to questions of 'fair', 'equitable','reasonable', or 'proper' shares in the joint results of occupational activities. The problem of 'justice' in the distribution of such shares is necessarily a *social* one. Nobody could argue about fair or unfair distributions unless a structure of groups whose members have similar interests within the group, but where the groups as such have conflicting interests, already exists.[1]

As far as the *pecuniary* side alone is concerned, the subject is

[1] For a more comprehensive treatment of this problem see T. H. Marshall (1950), pp. 71ff and *passim*.

traditionally covered by the theory of wages. There have been interminable controversies among economists over the analysis of wage-differentials in terms of marginal productivity. The intricate technicalities of these controversies have had the result that something far more important tends to be overlooked: the fact that there is a great deal of agreement over the more fundamental aspects of the occupational wage structure. This is the belief that although the labour market is capable of removing minor discrepancies in the wage structure, the larger occupational differentiations persist *for ever*. The notion of a permanent, immutable pyramid of occupational incomes is generally defended on economic grounds and is shared among professional economists, trade unionists, and employers alike.

There are, to be sure, certain variations in accepted terminology. Thus, economists usually describe the structure of wages as a 'natural' order. A particular wage-differential is 'distorted' when it does not reflect the distribution of labour resources derived from the existing pattern of 'inborn' abilities, intelligence levels, and acquired skills. The corresponding phraseology popular in trade union circles revolves round the principle of 'equity'; there is a slight difference here, in so far as differences in skill and training are more emphasized than innate abilities and propensities.

As the term 'equity' has played an increasingly important role in current wage policy, the time has come to remove its widely lamented vagueness. This can be done only by making its meaning more specific without, however, contradicting accepted usage. Considering the amount of confusion that has reigned in this field, the solution is fairly simple. What is generally accepted, though not clearly conceived, is the belief that the wage structure reflects, in the long run, differences in the relative scarcity of different types of labour resources. These are mainly due to the fact that there are large variations in the 'costs' involved in the acquisition of training, experience, and occupational education. In addition to this, variations in the natural endowment of special aptitudes, intelligence, and talent also affect the distribution of labour resources. Equity, in other

27

words, quite generally describes a wage structure that represents *lasting* differences in the relative scarcity of labour. The function of the labour market, then, is, according to the most widely accepted interpretation, to regulate the minor, short-term fluctuations in the supply and demand of labour in such a way that the permanent structure of equity remains.

One obvious source of such fluctuations is the change in productivity that comes from the product market. If the price for a given commodity rises because of an expanding market, the demand for labour in that industry, and therefore wages, will increase—temporarily. In due course more labour is attracted into the industry, and wages return to their previous level.

It is clear, then, that the fundamental problem lies in the more or less stable structure of equity, not in transitory and superficial adjustments. However, there may also be certain wage movements that are a result of changes neither in occupational costs nor in product prices. They may be due to trade-union action. In that case the usual argument is that the basic pattern of equitable differentials becomes permanently 'distorted' as a result of monopolistic pressures within the labour market caused by the rise of large and powerful unions. Thus, it is frequently thought that differences in the bargaining strength of particular unions, or sections within a union, will bring about lasting 'anomalies' in the wage structure. Similarly, the very technique of adjusting wage-claims may give rise to such distortions. For example, the favouring of flat-rate over proportionate wage increases for sectional wage demands, which developed with the trend towards industry-wide bargaining and the rise of mass unions, has frequently led to the levelling of wage differentials, chiefly with regard to skill (H. A. Turner (1952), pp. 227ff.). Nevertheless, it would obviously be wrong to assume that all organized pressure by workers on relative wages have, necessarily, a distorting effect. Clearly, there could also be *some* union actions that—far from creating artificial anomalies— actually reinforce or speed up processes that are on a par with the market mechanism. If, under certain conditions, the supply

28

of coal-miners becomes increasingly scarce, then their concerted action, implemented by strong organization, towards enforcing higher wages merely achieved what the market would do for them over a longer period. But no criteria have yet been discovered for deciding whether a particular union effect distorts or merely reinforces a given wage structure. Dissatisfactions with the promises of economic analysis in this field have increased in recent years. 'Do the changes of the past twenty years,' asks L. G. Reynolds, 'represent a correction of inequities which existed in pre-union days, or do they represent an additional distortion of the wage structure as the critics of unionism allege?... Who is to say what constitutes equity, or what is a "normal competitive relationship" among different wage rates?'[1]

It is indeed curious that no attempt has been made to look more closely into the nature of occupational costs as a possible determinant of equity. Any attempt of that kind would have revealed a difficulty far more profound than that associated with real or alleged anomalies in wage-differentials. It is by no means only an empirical difficulty. The measurement of major trends in occupational costs over certain periods would not be beyond the scope of existing data and statistical methods. But as soon as one starts reflecting on this possibility, a logical difficulty presents itself, which is insuperable. It stems from the fact that, for a very large working population, the occupational costs are *nil*, or very negligible. As far as most unskilled and semi-skilled wage-earners in factories and offices are concerned, investment in training and experience is so insignificant that it bears no relation to basic earnings. We are therefore forced to conclude that the wages of these groups are the compensation for something that has nothing to do with occupational costs. Let us call this factor the worker's input of '*effort*', provisionally defined as the sum total of physical and mental exertion, tedium, fatigue, or any other disagreeable aspect of work. It follows, on the basis of common knowledge, that this component must also be

[1] L. G. Reynolds, (1949), p. 408. Cp. also Louis R. Salkever (1953), p. 301f; F. Fürstenberg (1958), pp. 77–82.

29

present at all the higher levels of income, although it may differ widely between different levels of the occupational hierarchy. Furthermore, as it contains many subjective elements, this component defies rigorous definition and is certainly unmeasurable. Thus, a simple consideration of very obvious facts makes the principle of equity, as it stands at present, inapplicable to practical matters of wage policy. Clearly, it would be necessary to separate the two components of earned income: effort-compensation and occupational costs.

The only way of getting round this point would be to argue as follows. All that matters in respect of the controlling functions of the market are the relative changes through time; changes in occupational costs, effort, and incomes. Thus, in order to be able to ignore the effect of effort on income-differentials, we have only to assume that the effort component, though it may vary between different occupations, is constant over time: we do not need to know the absolute amount of effort required for different jobs, as long as the relative differences in effort do not change. Since this problem is never mentioned in current disputes over wage-differentials, some assumption of this sort may in fact be tacitly maintained. This is not perhaps unreasonable when comparing wages in very similar job situations. But if the assumption of constant effort proportions is also made for the analysis of earned income differentials between employers and employees, the approach becomes so abstract that it is almost meaningless. At the most one could then only say that the relationship between managerial incomes and wages, as controlled by the market, tends towards *some* degree of equity in terms of occupational-cost differentials. To *some* extent management would receive a relatively increasing share in the product if the costs of acquiring the skills of co-ordination (etc.) have increased, other things being equal. The extent would be unknown, since simultaneous changes in the effort component have to be ignored. This gap in the analysis is all the more disturbing, since it is the distribution of effort, rather than the structure of occupational costs, which is most relevant to the conflicting interests between employers and employees.

30

But the assumption of constant effort proportions is not only far-fetched where the really problematic aspects of industrial conflict are concerned. It is also absurd when we realize that it forces us to ignore another system of contractual controls that appears to operate side by side with the occupational market mechanism, though it is quite different from it. This is the system of administrative controls over the employee's efficiency. As it is a very complex apparatus, consisting of a large variety of methods generally believed to control the 'willingness to work', and therefore effort, it cannot be assumed away.

CHAPTER 3

Controls of Effort Stability

IT WILL not be possible to describe and to understand the administration of effort controls, unless we obtain first a clearer notion of what is commonly called 'efficiency'. This is not just a question of a more or less convenient terminology. Throughout the following discussion we shall not be merely concerned with the meaning of certain terms, although it may seem so at first. For the very process of administration itself is intrinsically tied up with the utilization of established language symbols and the values attached to them. The wholly tautological use of the words 'efficient' and (effective) 'administration' not only is characteristic of the bulk of the literature on the subject, both technical and popular, but also pervades the practical sphere. Equally characteristic is the curious fact that the term 'effort' and the problem of effort control tend to be avoided or neglected.

The assumption of unchanging effort proportions was introduced into modern economics by Alfred Marshall. It usually appears in the statement that the units of supply and demand, within each occupation and trade, must, on the average, be of 'equal efficiency'. The argument is that in the long run the extremes of under- and over-efficient persons are eliminated by the forces of competitive adjustments inherent in the market system, so that the units will be priced on the basis of some more or less average degree of efficiency. It has often been admitted that this concept cannot be rigorously defined because it involves subjective criteria. The occupational market, that is to say, the system of occupational controls, is thus envisaged as a very crude mechanism of control; it regulates quantities of people, not their productive quality. However, the patently obvious fact that in the real world there are marked variations in

32

efficiency within and between occupations could not be ignored. It has become the custom to associate—vaguely—these variations with all those techniques of administration which entrepreneurs and managers use to regulate the worker's efficiency. As this apparatus is clearly very formidable, and has been growing in importance with the modern trend towards large-scale operation, there is the possibility that the administrative control of efficiency duplicates, reinforces, or contradicts the functions of occupational controls. This may not be important in an economy of small and highly competitive firms that approximates fairly closely the theoretical model of an infinite number of self-employed producers. But when we approach the problem of large, complex industrial organizations, it becomes imperative to clarify the precise functions of efficiency controls.

As a first step, we shall substitute the term 'effort' for 'efficiency' control. Though neither word is in any way precise, the difference is nonetheless significant: by talking about 'effort' instead of 'efficiency', the range of relevant problems becomes distinctly narrower. Whereas 'effort' according to common sense is strictly limited to the human factor, the meaning of 'efficiency' is much wider because it frequently includes aspects of productivity that arise, independently of variations in effort, from the product market. This results from the general practice of measuring a firm's efficiency not only in terms of output per man, but also by recourse to variations in profits (defined as the difference between product prices and costs). As profits may go up or down simply as a reflex of changing product prices, such changes are of course irrelevant to the effectiveness of effort controls. Thus, by introducing the term 'effort', one large source of ambiguity, the double meaning of 'efficiency', has been eliminated.

It will further simplify our discussion if we reverse the usual assumptions. Instead of assuming constant effort proportions between occupations and status levels, we shall keep constant the proportions of occupational costs. This is justified by the obvious fact that the distribution of effort between employers and employees is far more relevant to the central problem of

33

differential shares in the product than the structure of occupational costs.

Despite these simplifications, the nature of effort controls is still very difficult to identify. They are as yet remarkably heterogeneous. They seem to cover anything from supervision, incentives, and profit-sharing to machine-paced production, methods of training, and employee-selection. They are used to increase output per man; to reduce absenteeism and labour turnover, to prevent strikes, to adjust wages, and so forth. For an analysis, as opposed to a common-sense description, it will have to be shown that there is some factor common to all effort controls, however diverse they may appear on the face of it to be. What, then, is this common denominator?

The question (barely even recognized as a problem in past research) is more baffling than one might expect. Let us first see if we can answer it by saying that they are methods of administration that entail a certain element of *coercion* and that it is in this that they differ from the occupational market, which turns on voluntarily contracted relations. Coercion, authority, discipline, and power have in fact been mentioned occasionally by some authors in this context. Thus, to repeat a phrase well known to economists, the business system, in contrast to the general market mechanism, has been described by D. H. Robertson as an 'island of conscious power' within an ocean of 'unconscious co-operation'.[1] One of the more obvious difficulties of using 'coercion' as a general criterion is the fact that among the most important administrative devices are financial incentives and the regulation of promotion. These are, in their effect, so similar to the stimulus inherent in ordinary market processes, so nearly an unconsciously operating control, that they do not seem to fit our criterion. And even if we take what is surely the most manifest case of administrative power, that is, close personal supervision, the problem is by no means simple.

It will be useful to look at supervision more carefully. We may

[1] D. H. Robertson (1923), p. 85. But the essentially non-coercive character of management and administration has also been much emphasized, e.g. see Herbert A. Simon (1946), p. 12 (and *passim*).

tentatively argue that supervision is a function that emerges immediately we take the first logical step towards the institution of employment. As soon as we have a division between employers and employees, rather than a system of single self-employed producers, there is a status differentiation between those who have authority and those who are subordinates. The command over employees implies an element of coerciveness that could possibly affect the division of the product between the two status positions. It is nevertheless true that supervision, even in this perspective, is nothing more than an extension—a refinement, as it were—of the occupational market system. The supervisor is merely engaged to ensure that the equation between the worker's input of effort and its equilibrium price in the form of wages is maintained. If there were no supervision (assuming perfect competition and mobility) it would be possible for some workers to reduce their effort temporarily, at a given level of wages. But eventually this would either impair the firm's competive position or attract more workers; in each case a re-adjustment of the balance between effort and its price must occur in the end. It is by means of constant supervision that this slow and wasteful process of eliminating 'inefficiency' is avoided.[1] It seems plausible, therefore, that the institution of employment with its supervisory controls is, in this respect, simply a superstructure that rests on the market mechanism. Moreover, it is possible to visualize the process of supervision as a method of bargaining between workers and supervisors (or managers); a method not fundamentally different from, though more flexible and rapid than, the crude regulation through the occupational market. This, in fact, is exactly what happens in reality; the formal wage contract is never precise in stipulating how much effort is expected for a given wage (and vice versa). The details of the arrangement are left to be worked out through the direct interaction between the partners of the contract. If a worker slackens his effort at one moment, the foreman's job is to remind him, as it were, that he departs from his obligations, and, in certain circumstances, it is quite possible that there may be some

[1] A somewhat similar argument has been put forward by R. H. Coase (1937).

35

haggling between the two as to what is a 'fair' degree of effort in relation to the wages paid. Even if an employee is dismissed for being inefficient, that, too, means that there was a discrepancy between the conduct expected under the arranged contract and its execution in terms of services actually rendered.

It can now be seen that *all* effort controls refine and elaborate the occupational controls of the market in the same sense. Supervision, as ordinarily understood, is only one example. Other managerial techniques such as payment by results, systems of promotion, merit-rating, job-evaluation, etc., though differing from personal supervision in some respects, have one function in common: that of keeping the employee's effort as closely as possible to the level for which the wage is paid. The method of piecework may be taken as another example. The most obvious advantage of piecework is that it requires less personal supervision than daywork. This is because under piecework the connection between effort and payment is automatically established and maintained. It follows that piecework is a further refinement of control compared with close supervision under daywork, just as supervision is an improvement on the market system.

Up to this point, the difference between occupational and effort controls seems a matter only of degree. There is, however, another difference that is more decisive. Essentially, the occupational market operates through *changes* of income differentials and thus changes in supply and demand. Supervision, piecework, etc., on the other hand, have the opposite effect: once they are established as a matter of routine, they *stabilize* the average level of individual effort over time. This is more obvious if we realize that the absolute amount of effort is unknown. Nor can anyone say what part of the wages is a reward for effort and what is a compensation for occupational costs. The employer (or supervisor), in trying to control effort, is merely guided by certain external manifestations of relative changes in effort, such as variations in output per man, quality of output, frequency of absence, level of discipline, etc. Once this is recognized, we can add one further type of effort controls: methods of machine-paced production, including the whole apparatus of flow production, which requires that the speed of work is stabilized through the interdependence of co-ordinated activities.

Thus, the stabilization of effort levels contrasts sharply with the general steering operation of the market. It involves the application of special managerial controls and the existence of a special authority, the firm. Though it is true that controls inside the firm to some extent repeat and articulate the commands of the market, they also achieve something else, and this is important. They stabilize activities in a highly standardized manner, thus removing from all bargaining and pricing processes fluctuations in behaviour that would otherwise result from immediate reactions to effort and income evaluations. It is therefore the stability function of effort controls that appears here as a separate mechanism, one that stands in its own right and can obviously not be treated as an insignificant duplication of the market mechanism. It is here that the greater coerciveness of control, as compared with the occupational market, is created. What is so coercive about these controls is precisely the psychological effect of effort routinization on the worker: the strain of being compelled to maintain a prescribed pace of work over indefinite periods. It should now also be clear that stability, as an independent element, grows in significance with increasing size and complexity of the firm. The more one approaches large-scale production, the more elaborate the arrangement of stabilizing controls becomes. All that is usually described as 'bureaucratization' of control contains this stabilizing element as a basis for predictability and calculability in industrial administration. It follows that the assumption of constant effort proportions, discussed earlier, is not altogether out of place. What is unrealistic about it is chiefly the belief that human nature and motivation is 'given' once and for all, without regard to the role of effort-stability controls.

It is evident that the provision of stability is a significant function of industrial administration. We have found that it is a function of effort controls and that it is this aspect which marks the difference between the system of effort administration and the system of occupational controls. One gap remains. Both systems are based on manifestations of human *behaviour*, which is objectively measurable in terms of indices of employee performance in the one case and numbers of people in the other. And yet it is clear from the foregoing that subjective conceptions of effort must somehow intrude into both types of control. However intangible, they cannot be taken for granted. Otherwise the distribution of differential shares in the proceeds of industry between management and workers, and thus the nature of industrial conflict, would remain as inexplicable as ever. This problem does not necessarily arise in any specific form in the routine of administrative practice. There, apparently, it seems sufficient, as a rule, to proceed on the strength of intuitive guesses about variations in human 'efficiency' and, for the rest, to rely on measurement of performance and numbers of people.

CHAPTER 4

Controls of Effort Intensity

WE MUST now clarify the statement that, as far as is known, rough guesses about effort usually seem to provide sufficient guide for administration. If one glances superficially at any one of the various techniques of effort-stability control, it is true that objective records of employee performance (output, attendance, and so on) are the main source of information. But it is only true as long as the situation does not undergo any major changes. Let us suppose a firm is rapidly expanding and wants to introduce new methods of production. New skills, different types of worker, and changes in method of payment will be required. Obviously, in working out new routines of stability-control, the question of effort-input in relation to wages becomes unavoidable. For instance, before output per man-hour can be used as a measure of efficiency on a new process, there must be some notion about the minimum speed of work necessary to cover costs, and for this an estimate of the worker's effort is indispensable. Thus, either something better than intuitive judgements must be available, or the whole administration of industrial change rests on a highly irrational element. The same applies to the employee himself. He, too, must estimate the intensity of effort that will be expected from him in a changing situation. Unfortunately, the problem has been covered up by the universally accepted supposition, apparently ineradicable, that wage-earners are irrationally hostile to all technological and organizational innovations on account of sheer 'conservatism'.

None of these questions can be answered straightaway. We shall continue, in this chapter, without an analytical definition of effort. It will nevertheless be possible to identify in addition to stability-control another function of industrial administration: the control of effort-*intensity*. This function may easily be

D

misunderstood because it has two aspects: (a) one and the same technique, such as payment by results, may be used either to stabilize a given level of effort or to increase the intensity of effort; that is to say, a particular method of administration has alternative uses. (b) It is also possible that there are specific devices for each function. To simplify the discussion, the second case will be considered first.

The possibility of deliberately manipulating the intensity of employee effort is a relatively new problem which quite generally concerns the motivation to work. Judging from popular writings, examples of this type of administration are at first not very striking. Such methods as employee counselling, group discussions, joint consultation, works information, and staff-upgrading are frequently mentioned, but little is said of their effectiveness in controlling effort. The emphasis is put, rather, on the underlying emotions: team spirit, identification, self-expression, and so forth. Such sentiments are very different from the economic motives connected with conventional administration. They may be effective without being conscious. They may not have a physiological basis. Moreover, it seems feasible that such emotions may be shaped, adjusted, or even created, in the very process of applying the appropriate techniques of control. It is claimed, for instance, that the purpose of joint discussions in works committees is not only to alleviate the worker's dissatisfactions, but also to act as a therapeutic release mechanism for 'tensions', bringing them into the open and as a result making the worker identify himself more closely with the aims of the organization. It is thought that methods of this kind, if successful, might create, even in large-scale bureaucratic organizations, a psychological atmosphere of common endeavour and team spirit.[1] Clearly, these new devices of control cannot adequately be understood as a mechanical stimulus to existing motives, as is the case with incentive schemes and disciplinary sanctions. The total situation is so handled as to condition the employee to the desirable frame of mind, rather than to stimulate him to

[1] Elliott Jaques (1951), pp. 85, 88, 249, 306ff. A particularly informative study of the new manipulative techniques is presented by Norman R. F. Maier (1952).

40

perform specific actions. And it is not the objective external situation that is manipulated, but the employee's subjective definition of it.

But the concept of manipulation also implies 'power exercised unbeknown to the manipulated'.[1] Since in a sense this contradicts the general belief in the inviolability of an individual's volition and emotion, it will not easily be accepted as a valid description of the new techniques of effort-intensity control. I therefore wish to add further illustrations. The technical literature on group dynamics and human relations in industry reveals sufficient evidence on this point, though it is rarely explicitly recognized.[2] The importance of manipulation has already clearly been emphasized by Chester Barnard ((1938), p. 141): 'An organization can secure the efforts necessary to its existence, then, either by the objective inducements it provides or by changing *states of mind*'. Roethlisberger and Dickson (1939, p. 592 and p. 602) describe the purpose of employee counselling by stating that: 'the interview is a diagnostic and therapeutic tool . . .'; the counsellor 'directs the employee's *thinking* into those areas which he needs to take into account to achieve an adequate adjustment'. More recently we are told by Charles R. Walker (1950, p. 54) that changes in work methods in a highly mechanized plant, described as 'job-enlargement', resulted in an 'increase in personal *satisfaction* for each of the participants'. Similarly, according to H. A. Simon (1947, p. 11), '. . . the behaviour of the operative employee can be influenced . . . by establishing in the operative employee himself *attitudes*, habits and a *state of mind* which lead him to reach that decision which is advantageous to the organization . The same notion is expressed by Norman R. F. Maier (1952, p. VII), in connection with employee training: 'One must not only have effective

[1] C. Wright Mills (1949), pp. 214f. To my knowledge the first penetrating insight into industrial manipulation has come from C. Wright Mills. The concept goes back to H. Goldhamer and Edward A. Shils (1939), p. 172. Cp. now also David Riesman (1950), pp. 311ff.

[2] I have therefore italicized, in the following quotations, such words as point to manipulation of motives and sentiments. For further examples see C. Wright Mills (1949), to which the present analysis owes a great deal.

procedures to offer, but one must also *motivate* people to use the effective procedures that are available. . . . It requires changes in established habits as well as changes in *attitudes*.'

All these statements are strongly coloured by a belief in the superior effectiveness of manipulative skills and methods of control, and since they are expressed from either practical experience or close contact with industrial management, the contrast to traditional methods, where motives were simply taken for granted, seems real enough. Nevertheless, the actual scope for changing an employee's motives appears to be rather narrow. The relevant studies usually admit that their conclusions are subject to various limitations. Sentiments as such cannot be measured, and the effectiveness of the techniques that attempt to change them can only be inferred from overt behaviour. 'Other things' never remain constant, for instance, methods of production, stability controls, or the situation in the labour market. This even applies to conditions that resemble a controlled experiment, as is clearly admitted by Roethlisberger and Dickson.[1] Or it is found that it has not, in fact, been possible to increase the worker's satisfaction (D. Cox and K. M. Dyce, 1951). And in some cases where successful manipulation of 'morale' is claimed, it is not made clear to what extent this was in fact due to changes in environment, for instance by setting up a plant in an area where trade unions are weak or the level of employment is relatively low.

The manipulation of effort-intensity is, however, not necessarily restricted to methods having no other purpose. There are certain techniques of control that potentially affect both the intensity and the stability of effort. An example is industrial training. Avowedly, its primary aim is to inculcate habits of work that will result in a more stable and predictable performance. However, while this improves the stability of effort, a change in the attitude to the job situation also occurs.[2] The

[1] '. . . the condition that all other things remain the same had failed of realization (1939), p. 158).

[2] The effect of training and education on attitudes is generally recognized; cp. the quotation from N. R. F. Maier on p. 47 above. Further evidence is given by T. A. Ryan and P. Cain Smith (1954), p. 429.

trainee gradually becomes interested in the operation and derives certain satisfactions from the skill or the dexterity it demands, and the promise of improved status that the new job
may hold out for him probably adds to these sentiments;
furthermore, if the training is carried out within an established
company training scheme, one may expect some positive effect
on the trainee's attitude to the firm, in terms of increased identification. Training may thus be considered as a method of manipulation that involves both stability and intensity-control of
effort.

Another example of a method that includes both aspects is
the application of payment by results. The most obvious function is, as mentioned in the previous chapter, the stabilization of
effort levels once such a method has been established as a fixed
routine. The manipulation of effort-intensity is here, however,
not much in evidence because it is concealed behind the technicalities of rate-setting by means of which an agreed relation
between wage rates and specific standards of effort is obtained.[1]
Before a particular system of wage payment can be permanently
arranged, a definite relationship between rates and effort must
be secured. Both are intended to move towards a higher level.
It is therefore the *introduction* of incentives, the changeover from
daywork to piecework, which requires a control over effort-
intensity and thus a manipulation of attitudes.

A few quotations, chosen at random, may illustrate this
point. The survey of payment by results published by the I.L.O.
(1951) contains a whole chapter on 'Procedures Used in Introducing and Applying Systems of Payment by Results'. It emphasizes that 'the first requirement for the success of a system of
payment by results is that it should be developed and applied
with the agreement of the workers concerned and in an atmosphere of good industrial relations' (p. 31). Similarly, a leading
textbook on personnel administration speaks of the 'fundamental principle' that the introduction of changes in payment methods must be jointly determined by employers and

[1] Only a brief account of this process is necessary at present; the problem will
be further discussed in Chapter 9.

employees in order to be 'successful' (Tead and Metcalf (1933), p. 249, pp. 304ff.). The British Institute of Management emphasizes that 'unless mutual confidence and good relations exist between Management and Workers in a concern, the chance of full success for a new wage incentive system is very poor' (B. I. M. (1950), p. 5). Similar statements could be quoted *ad libitum*. They express what is, undoubtedly, a generally held opinion.[1]

It is also well known that 'success' in terms of relatively increased effort is often due to a period of induction during which the new system is put on trial, carefully explained and possibly made a subject for joint consultation. A striking example of the importance of rate-setting in this context is the building industry, where the traditional hostility of the workers against incentive systems had to be 'bought off' by granting generous increases in basic rates.[2] But although the overall importance of changing attitudes is generally acknowledged, the specific role of manipulation as a method of persuasion is barely recognized. This is not perhaps surprising, for incentives and rate-setting are the subject-matter of production engineers, who are neither particularly interested in nor equipped to deal with that aspect. Social psychologists, on the other hand, do not usually feel competent to deal with the technicalities of production engineering. And both aspects seem equally irrelevant to economics.

This may explain why the fact that even the purely technical side of time-and-motion study cannot be logically separated from the problem of wage adjustments is always overlooked. Though the time-study practitioner will usually time a job without thinking about wages, he must somehow relate effort to 'efficiency'; and ultimately either he, or someone in the wage department, must determine what is the most efficient level of effort for a given wage rate, or what should be paid for a given standard of effort. There are always at least three interdependent

[1] Investigations on incentives in special industries are also relevant here, for example: George P. Shultz (1951), pp. 107–198; V. L. Allen (1952); J. Crawford (1953), pp. 231ff.; Ministry of Works (1947).
[2] V. L. Allen (1952) pp. 595ff.; C. A. Mace (1950), N. Davis (1948).

44

variables involved in the situation: a conception of effort intensity, a rate of pay, and a method of production. If the method of work is altered (if, for instance, less skill is required), both the operator and the time-study man expect that either pay or effort, or both, will also change. If we keep the methods of production constant, to simplify matters, it will be possible for a worker to vary intensity of effort according to this conception of what is tolerable or worthwhile, and he will do so in response to any change in the rate of pay. The most familiar illustration of this is restriction of output. Similarly the employer, represented by the time-study man, must endeavour to adjust wage rates to any change in the worker's exertion. Here the most important process is 'rate-cutting'. In other words, no matter what happens, *some* relation between effort and pay must be in the minds of those who control the situation.

There is plenty of evidence in all publications and discussions on the practical success of time-study and work measurement that it is necessary to discover the prevailing notions of the 'right' level of effort *'required'* in a particular situation. The success, indeed the very possibility of systematic time-study, including the more sophisticated methods of work measurement, rest entirely on the existence of such preconceptions. Most of the paraphernalia of 'scientific' measurement and accuracy are unimportant details. Fundamentally, the whole process is a matter of intuitive judgement, based on long experience, training, close familiarity with the technical and human aspects of the situation, and a great deal of common sense. Whether one is successful or not in finding the 'required' standard times depends decisively upon the discovery of the preconceived, habitually maintained standards of normal exertion in any type of operation. The true purpose of scientific objectivity in the practice of work measurement is precisely the opposite of what it claims to be in theory: though precision and consistency in the form of technical terms and measuring appliances are indispensable, and even important, they have the function, not of eliminating the intrusion of effort conceptions, *but, on the contrary*, of detecting and making them all the more amenable to consistent

45

guesswork. The true purpose of time-study, in other words, is to guess as consistently as possible the purely subjective element of effort standards, and subsequently to adjust rates of pay in accordance with them. Moreover, the very act of timing a job may raise the acceptable level of effort. Thus, to be more precise, we can say that the object of the rate-setting process is to discover the *upper limit* of tolerable effort, this is, the highest standard that can subsequently be maintained without restriction of output or strained industrial relations.

In practice, all these matters are closely intertwined. The introduction of incentives is inseparable from the rate-setting process, and the evaluation of effort is inescapably linked to the firm's wage policy. Simultaneously, there are changes in methods of production and in the composition of personnel. But, nevertheless, these things can also be taken apart analytically. If the empirical observations so far available do not always appear to permit this, one can at least tell which way the emphasis points. Thus we have seen that incentives on the whole point towards control of stabilized effort levels, once they are an established routine. Rate-setting, especially when connected with changeover from daywork to incentives, is predominantly a problem of effort-intensity control. This last point particularly deserves attention, for it shows that the modern trend towards an increasing preoccupation with human relations in industry cannot be dismissed as something having little to do with the central issues of industrial relations—the problems of effort in relation to income differentials.

In summing up the results of Part I, it should be recalled that I have tried to cover as large a variety of regulative controls as possible within the limitations of available theory and research. As the problems that have emerged in the course of the discussions are partially unsolved, a distinction between what is now reasonably certain and what still remains for further analysis seems indicated.

1. We have found that there are three markedly different types of contractual regulation: occupational controls, effort-stability controls, and the manipulation of effort-intensity. In

starting off with certain defects in the present system of industrial organization (such as permanent occupational instability), we discovered a peculiar gap in the system of occupational controls; the unknown costs of human effort in relation to occupational costs. The gap is concealed by the usual assumption of constant effort proportions. The same problem reappeared in the discussion of effort-stability controls. These are based merely on criteria of employee performance, while the underlying standards of effort are assumed as given or unchanging. Finally, with effort-intensity controls, the dominant aim is to increase the degree of effort which the employee is expected to surrender to the firm.

2. Despite its importance, the substance of effort is always unknown and its manifestations are intangible. Apart from intuitive judgements, there is no determinate relation between effort levels and wage payment. It can be said therefore that the entire complex of contractual controls rests, strategically, on a factor that has so far been inaccessible. Our next task is to concentrate on the analytical components of this factor.

PART II

Industrial Motivation

THE MEANING OF EFFORT

CHAPTER 5

Impairment and Inurement

ALTHOUGH conceptions of effort undoubtedly pervade the whole sphere of industrial organization, we know very little about them. As a first approximation, they seem to consist of various sentiments that are connected with deterrents to industrial work. Economists have occasionally felt the need to take an interest in these matters, but they have, in fact, always treated such phenomena as 'fatigue', 'unrest', and 'boredom' on a common-sense level, without coming anywhere near a definition of them. As regards industrial sociology, the problem has been avoided until very recently. The only field where sustained research has been done on deterrents is industrial psychology. Investigations on fatigue and boredom, for example, have a long and continuous history going back to the beginning of this century.

It is a history distinguished by a cumulative progress in methods and scope of inquiry, ranging from rigorous laboratory tests to realistic field experiments. But this development was brought to a stop in 1947 by a profoundly disturbing discovery. Arthur Ryan, an industrial psychologist, who had himself previously worked on tests of fatigue, demonstrated the existence of tacit assumptions within the conceptual framework of industrial psychology.[1] He found, in particular, that the subjective-motivational aspect of effort, as an important determinant of labour efficiency, had been completely overlooked by many psychologists. The problem had either been ignored, or it was assumed, without evidence, that effort (and similar phenomena such as fatigue) is a linear function of the physical energy consumed in working. Ryan concluded that effort can only be

[1] T. A. Ryan (1947). Cp. also T. A. Ryan and P. Cain Smith (1954), pp. 353ff.

51

described introspectively; it cannot be measured by any available tests.

In facing up to this position, one must be fully aware of the subjective element in deterrents. When one talks, in ordinary language, about 'deterrents to work', the external and objectively observable environment of work is easily confused with the subjective feelings such an environment arouses. For example, work 'monotony' may refer *either* to the repetitive nature of an activity *or* to the concurrent feeling of boredom. To emphasize the difference, I shall contrast, throughout what follows, objective '*work realities*' with subjective '*work deprivations*'. The latter are the psychological response to the former. It will be seen that there are several types of deterrent and that in each case it is possible to distinguish these two aspects.

There is, however, an additional complication that must be removed to simplify the discussion. Work realities cover all the technological and organizational factors that shape the immediate environment of productive activity. Obviously, some of these factors (such as extremely hard work) will not only arouse certain feelings of deprivation, but will also have some physiological effects. It is possible, on the other hand, that the physiological processes are unknown or perhaps do not even exist. This problem can be omitted, since for our purpose it is unimportant whether the physiological basis of a given deprivation is known or not. The relevant point is that even if such feelings have no apparent physiological basis, there still has to be a set of work realities with which they are associated.

It need hardly be stressed that the description of work deprivations depends largely on introspection. If, however, one always attempts to connect a particular emotion with a specific work reality, the description will be less impressionistic. We shall find, moreover, that everyday words are more useful for introspective descriptions than they may seem, provided that the unique character of industrial work is borne in mind. Thus, as Mace (1905b), and others before, have pointed out, the difficulty lies, not in the use of introspection, but in the translation of special experiences into universal valid terms. In the following passages, the technical terms I use are intended to cover the sentiments of the wage-earners only, unless special reference is made to professional or other types of work.

Another difficulty is that feelings of deprivation, even when clearly associated with specific work realities, are often ambivalent. Hard work, for instance, is not necessarily reflected in feelings of discomfort only. It can also produce certain satisfactions. As a matter of fact, all work deprivations may be connected with what I shall call 'relative satisfactions'.[1] They are feelings of temporary relief from the discomfort of certain work realities, feelings which arise when these factors have become part of the workers' customary interpretation of his situation. They are, to this extent, only apparent satisfactions, which are actually derived from deprivation.

The most familiar work deprivation is the experience of physical *impairment*. It is the state of mind of a person aware of his physical discomfort caused by strenuous work. In extreme cases, heavy work over long hours would be an obvious work reality corresponding to this state of mind. But to obtain a wider application, we have to include here under work realities all that is conventionally summarized as 'physical conditions' of work: heat, cold, noise, dampness, dirtiness, as well as hours of work.

On the face of it, one might expect there to be a lot of information available on impairment as a deterrent to work. But although there are numerous investigations on the subject (formerly called 'fatigue' in a very wide sense), little is known about the nature and effects of impairment as a factor in motivation.[2] The main reason that so little is known of how workers experience impairment is that the objective of past research has been confined to the efficiency of work—'efficiency' as conceived by

---

[1] To put it more generally, they are a case of 'substitute goals'; cf. Kurt Lewin (1935), p.108ff.; Anna Freud (1937); J. C. Flugel (1945) Chap. VI. The concept of 'relative deprivation', developed in *The American Soldier*, covers virtually the same phenomenon. See S. A. Stouffer, E. A. Suchman, *et al.*, vol. I (1949), pp. 125ff.; Robert K. Merton and Alice S. Kitt (1950), pp. 51ff.

[2] There are two surveys which, between them, virtually cover the whole ground of fatigue investigations: Bartley and Chute (1947) and T .A. Ryan (1947).

the employer. The tradition has been, with rare exceptions,[1] to determine the marginal effect of working conditions (for instance, hours of work) on productivity, with a view to finding optimum conditions. But this contributes little to the motivational aspects of industrial work. Moreover, so far it has not been specifically recognized that the feeling of impairment tends to be overlaid by relative satisfactions connected with it. What people think or feel about their working conditions depends to a large extent on what I propose to call 'psychological inurement'[2] By this I refer, first of all, to the common-sense observation that people, in the course of time, seem to get used to almost any condition they are forced or induced to tolerate. As regards industrial environments, we find numerous scattered observations, chiefly on noise, heat, and light, which, if taken as a whole, leave no doubt that initially unpleasant or irritating conditions loose their effect after some time.[3] Heat and noise that seem excessive to the newcomer, do not appear to worry the veteran worker. Various expressions are used in the literature for such observations, e.g. acclimatization, adaptation, habituation, and adjustment—all meaning that the response to a given stimulus becomes progressively weaker if the stimulus is continually and unvaryingly repeated. However, it still remains uncertain, so far, how much the apparently physiological causes of inurement are in fact the result of a changed attitude, or at least reinforced by concurrent psychological processes. For the available evidence has come to light mostly as a by-product of investigations primarily concerned with physiological working capacity and efficiency; the gradual wearing-off of a changed condition in such experiments is likely to be regarded as a secondary, if not an undesired element, in so far as it is due to psychological

[1] N. Balchin (1947); Norah Davis (1953), pp. 25f; Charles R. Walker (1954), C. von Ferber (1959).

[2] For lack of a better term, I am taking the translation of the German *Gewöh-nung*, used first by E. Kraepelin (1902). See also Max Weber (1908–9), p. 758, Georg Simmel (1950) pp. 382f, and G. Friedmann (1960) p. 346.

[3] For example, Wyatt, Fraser, and Stock (1929), p. 38: 'Situations which, at the outset, may be very unpleasant because of the tedium and strain they produce, are afterwards endured without complaint, and in some cases with a certain amount of enjoyment'. Cf. also Weston and Adams (1932), pp. 38ff.

effects. Special attention has only been given to inurement with regard to noise.[1]

But although we have no study on the specifically psychological aspect of inurement, the impression that physical conditions are, on the whole, subjectively not very important to the seasoned worker is indirectly supported by statistics on labour turnover. It has been known for some time,[2] and confirmed again and again in recent studies, that newcomers have the highest turnover rates; as length of service increases, turnover rates decline consistently (other things being equal).

In the study by J. Long it appears that there is some tendency for labour turnover to be raised by noisy conditions coupled with dirt—but only among workers with fairly short periods of service (see *Table 4*, p. 56). Factories D.1 and D.3 each employed women in their manufacturing departments where there was a great deal of noise and the work was dirty. Women were also employed in the sorting and wrapping departments where conditions were quiet and clean. The table shows that women with less than five years' service had much higher controllable turnover rates in each factory's manufacturing departments than in its sorting and wrapping departments, but the controlled turnover of the long-service workers seemed to bear no relation to the physical conditions in the departments. Thus it seems that whereas some workers cannot tolerate noise and dirt, or leave before they begin to, others either are unaffected by it from the beginning or become accustomed to it. Probably many workers can adjust themselves in this way, for the proportion of long-service workers in the manufacturing departments was high.

To sum up: as far as motivation is concerned, not much is known about impairment as a psychological response to the physical conditions of work, but it seems probable that impairment tends to be mitigated by relative satisfactions in the form of inurement.

---

[1] Cp. the admirable review and criticism of past research by T. A. Ryan (1947), pp. 124ff.

[2] Joyce R. Long (1951), pp. 52ff., 111ff.; Hilde Behrend (1953), pp. 69ff.; A. K Rice, J. M. M. Hill, and E. L. Trist (1950), pp. 349–72.

E

56

TABLE 4   DIFFERENCES IN LABOUR TURNOVER BETWEEN DEPARTMENTS WITH DIFFERING PHYSICAL WORKING CONDITIONS*

| | FACTORY D.1 | | | | | | FACTORY D.3 | | | | | |
| | Manufacturing | | Sorting | | Wrapping | | Manufacturing | | Sorting | | Wrapping | |
Length of Service	Employed Dec. 1948	Controllable turn-over	Employed Dec. 1948	Controllable turn-over	Employed Dec. 1948	Controllable turn-over	Employed Dec. 1948	Controllable turn-over	Employed Dec. 1948	Controllable turn-over	Employed Dec. 1948	Controllable turn-over
		%		%		%		%		%		%
Less than 5 years	22	77	70	44	54	24	19	84	66	48	24	33
5 years and over	77	14	65	11	36	8	95	2	37	14	36	6
Total	99	28	135	28	90	18	114	16	103	40	60	17

* Source: Joyce R. Long (1951).

CHAPTER 6

Tedium and Traction

UNDER modern conditions of mass production, the most pertinent work reality is the high degree of repetitiveness of light work. What is usually described as 'boredom' is more conspicuous here than impairment. A few observations are fairly well established, particularly with regard to individual differences in susceptibility to boredom. But many questions remain as baffling as they were some 40 years ago when Münsterberg first started to distinguish boredom from fatigue (impairment). Above all, there is no answer to the question, admittedly not a simple one, as to what the nature of boredom is. As T. A. Ryan (1947, p. 202) sums up the problem: 'the only method of gauging the tendency to boredom in a given worker is to question him as carefully as possible.' But to be able to ask fruitful questions, the investigator himself must first have some idea of what is specific to *industrial* boredom; to use an introspective notion derived from his own professional work is obviously not very helpful, and may indeed falsify the whole approach from the start. For it is possible that the repetition worker's experience of boredom is of quite a different nature from that connected with professional work. The academic person, for instance, is bored by a technical book if its subject-matter has no connection with his particular sphere of interests. This has nothing to do with repetition. I therefore suggest that the term 'boredom' be reserved for professional occupations and 'tedium' for the corresponding sentiment in repetition work.

In describing the feeling of tedium on the basis of what is generally known from published reports,[1] the most important

[1] I am also drawing upon my own experience, which is based not on participant observation, but on a period of five years of ordinary employment as a manual worker. The most repetitive job of which I have personal experience as well as information from workers is the labelling of cartons. The work cycle is about 0.7 seconds.

feature seems to me to be its instability. Unlike impairment, it is not a condition that appears in a fairly predictable manner after a certain time and increases its intensity with increased activity. Moreover, it cannot easily be separated from other causes of discomfort. Nor has it been possible to find a definite relationship between the degree of repetition measured by the time normally taken by a trained worker to complete one work cycle, and the intensity of the feeling. This is largely due to the impossibility of isolating the degree of repetition from other characteristics of the activity. If, to accentuate the phenomenon, operations with greatly differing length of cycle are compared, these will be jobs which are qualitatively so different that sentiments and feelings other than tedium are bound to interfere. By comparing very similar activities with but a slight variation in cycle time, the matter becomes so subtle that no noticeable difference in intensity of tedium is felt.

There is one point, however, which does lead us a little further. In operations such as press-operating, simple inspection, assembling, labelling, machine-feeding, etc., which are intermittent, so that each cycle appears as a separate act, it appears that the discomfort of tedium is noticeably greater between two cycles than in the course of the cycle operation. More effort seems to be required to start a new cycle than to conclude one already in process. This suggests that tedium is primarily connected with the mental effort required to join two consecutive cycles. It would follow that the shorter the unit cycle, the greater (per day or hour) is the number of inter-cycle decisions required for a continuous performance, and hence, probably, the greater the tedium. But the word 'decision' should not be taken too literally, for in any routine operation the whole thing is semi-automatic.

The impression that it is more tedious to join than to complete separate cycles has some support from the experiments on satiation carried out by Anitra Karsten.[1] They consisted, briefly, of asking various subjects to cover pieces of paper with pencil

[1] Kurt Lewin and Anitra Karsten (1928), pp. 142–254. These experiments have been repeated under the direction of Robert B. MacLeod by B. I. M. Bews (1951). I am greatly indebted to Miss Bews for providing me with detailed information about the proceedure and the results of the experiment.

58

strokes in certain patterns. After a period, when a stage of satiation was reached, several subjects found that it was relatively more painful to start a new page than to complete one already started. Although they are not sufficiently comparable with industrial conditions, these experiments are illuminating for another reason. They indicated that satiation is strongly dependent on motivational projections; with subjects who thought the experiment served some important purpose, the onset of satiation was delayed, whereas those who interpreted the experiments as meaningless from the start, experienced greater discomfort. The crucial role of motivation emerged also in the fact that the feelings expressed were highly unstable.

Returning to industrial repetitive tasks, there is no doubt that workers do associate a feeling of tedium with highly monotonous operations, although on the whole it is only a feeling of a mild discomfort which has no apparent relationship with the degree of repetition. The surprising absence of severe distress (such as has occurred in experimental situations) has often been commented upon. It will therefore be our main task to look out for all those relative satisfactions which are likely to overlay, postpone, or remove any very acute experience of tedium. This means that the specific work reality, repetitiveness, would produce the severely painful experience of satiation only if there were no concurrent satisfactions.

The strongest and most frequent of these relative satisfactions is what, in an earlier study, I have called 'traction'[1] because, in a sense, it is the opposite of 'dis-traction'. It is a feeling of being pulled along by the inertia inherent in a particular activity. The experience is pleasant and may therefore function as a relief from tedium. It usually appears to be associated, though not always, with a feeling of reduced effort, relative to actual or imagined situations where it is difficult to maintain continuity of performance.

[1] I first described the phenomenon of traction in a monograph (Baldamus (1951a)) which is now out of print. The substance of it is recorded by T. A. Ryan and P. Cain Smith (1954) pp. 383–6; experiences similar to traction have been described as 'self-sustaining tendencies' by J. C. Flugel (1947). I am indebted to Norah Davis for this reference.

Traction seems closely related to 'rhythm' which is a better-known phenomenon because it is familiar from common experience. Rhythm in work was first extensively described by the historian Karl Bücher (1919, pp. 24ff; p. 366), who was fully aware of the effort-reducing character of rhythm. But his observations were only descriptive and based chiefly on non-industrial work. The importance of rhythm as an effort-reducing factor also occurs in specific industrial activities; this is indicated by numerous chance observations, particularly in some of the reports by the Industrial Health Research Board. In studies on variety in work it was found that frequent changes from one operation to another reduced the rate of output owing to the interference with the 'swing of work' (H. M. Vernon, S. Wyatt, and A. D. Ogden (1924), pp. 17 and 22). A comparison of the work curves of handkerchief folding and ironing in a laundry showed a regular fall of the curve in the case of folding but a remarkable rise throughout the spell for ironing; this was tentatively explained by a 'natural rhythm' inherent in ironing (S. Wyatt and J. A. Fraser (1925), pp. 19ff). S. Wyatt repeatedly refers to similar observations in a number of studies on repetitive work. For instance, a lathe, 'when running, exerts a pull which impels the operative to keep going even when fatigued...' (S. Wyatt and J. N. Langdon (1938), p. 44).

However, most of these observations were interpreted by reference to the concept of capacity to work. It was, therefore, an important change of orientation when attention was first directed to the fact that emotional attitudes to work may be a crucial factor in the relation between output and effort. This step was taken in the course of a study by Wyatt on Incentives in Repetitive Work.[1] If it is true that such phenomena as 'rhythm', 'swing', and 'pull' affect effort at work, different types of work must produce different reactions on the part of the worker. The study compares (under controlled conditions) five repetitive, outwardly very similar, operations connected with the packing of toffees and chocolates: wrapping, unwrapping, packing (into

[1] Wyatt and others (1934); see also Ryan's discussion of this study (1947), pp. 185f.

tins), weighing, and weighing combined with wrapping. It was found that the various types of work produced marked differences in the worker's attitudes and patterns of behaviour. This was closely related to variations in the rate of improvement during the learning period. During this period, which lasted altogether 35 weeks, the external incentive pressure was twice stepped up, from daywork to bonus rate and then to piece-rate. Of the five operations, wrapping showed the greatest improvement, while there was practically no change in the output rate of unwrapping. The other operations took an intermediate position both in order of preference and relative improvement.

Much of the explanation offered to account for the differences in emotional attitude and performance is clearly relevant to the elements of traction inherent in the various operations, or alternatively to interferences with traction. Unwrapping was disliked by the workers partly because of 'the tendency of the paper to stick to the toffee'. Of weighing, which was disliked almost as much as unwrapping, it was said that 'the short but frequent interruptions caused by inserting paper slips in the tins and the packing of the tins in cartons was annoying because they interfered with the main operation'. Wrapping was performed with 'rapidity and ease' and was 'free from interruptions and variations so that the operatives were able to adopt a rhythmical method of work' (ibid. p. 26).

Similarly, 'the statements of the operatives contained many references to minor features of the work which were regarded as annoying interruptions because they interfered with the continuity of the processes and impeded progress' (S. Wyatt *et al.* (1934), p. 27); or 'the annoyance caused whenever the cycles of movement were interrupted or impaired was intensified by occasional defects in the material' (ibid.). So numerous are such references that one wonders whether a common source for these irritations may not be found in specific elements of the external working situation. The answer is, I think, that they stem from imperfections in the routine pattern of production, imperfections that interfere with the expectation of traction.

It will help further analysis if we obtain a mental image of

61

traction that is sufficiently meaningful to permit the comparison of different situations. The following types of traction may be distinguished.[1]

Object traction. This kind of traction is also experienced in many non-industrial activities and is therefore more easily recognized by those who are not familiar with manual industrial work. The experience derives mainly from visualizing an object or its parts which one feels urged to reproduce or complete. It is found in many hobby activities such as modelling, carpentry, painting. In industrial work its most powerful form exists in crafts that are concerned with making things. A single press-tool may occupy the toolmaker for a period of 4 to 6 weeks. During this time the object is mentally, and to some extent actually, divided up into separate stages and parts, and it is first of all the desired shape of a part that exercises traction on the worker. A picture of the whole product is, however, also present in his mind, and this added element of traction increases in intensity as the job nears completion. In labelling cartons, though object traction is present, it is very weak indeed. The object is one labelled carton, and traction is experienced during each work cycle. Its effect becomes noticeable when irritating obstacles interfere with the smooth run of the cycle. The comparison between tool-making and labelling shows that the two jobs do not differ only in tedium. The chief difference derives from the different intensity of object traction, apart from the contrast in respect of tedium.

Batch traction. Many operations in industry are subject to a type of traction that is connected with a desire to complete a batch of articles. This too is well illustrated by the case of labelling. The feeling of traction is stronger when the completion of the batch is approaching. It is known from various studies on repetitive work that subdividing a large number of articles or components into smaller groups helps to diminish the feeling of tedium.[2] This phenomenon is also related to

[1] The illustrations chosen are based on self-observation.

[2] Experiments by P. Cain Smith and C. Lem (1953), have produced some evidence to support this.

observations on the beneficial influence of 'knowledge of re-sults' (C. A. Mace, 1935).

Process traction. This is experienced in operations where the tempo and sequence of the motions are determined by the chemical or physical nature of the production process, as is the case in melting, casting, glass-blowing, soldering, welding, painting, chocolate-dipping, forging, spraying, etc. However, it should not be thought that the movements of the operator are simply forced on him. There is usually a distinctly pleasant sensation in being guided or pulled along by the process in completing a given work cycle. Frequently, process traction is combined with object traction, for example, in glass-blowing.

Machine traction. Operations on machines which are constantly running produce in the operator the feeling of being drawn along. To isolate machine traction, care must be taken to put object traction out of one's mind, as this usually occurs simultaneously. For instance, in turning a steel bar along a given distance, there is a pull towards completing each run in one movement, even before the desired thickness is approached; although in the first stages of the operation the worker could, if he wanted, interrupt the action without damage to the finished product, there is a tendency to extend the continuous operation as long as possible. Thus, he feels inclined to keep going with repeated cycles while the machine is running.

Line-traction. Modern methods of flow production are char-acterized by the same object passing through a series of oper-ations which are carried out by different workers, with or with-out the help of a conveyor belt. Usually a strong movement of traction is inherent in such methods of production. But it is not easily recognized because most outside observers associate work on a conveyor belt with a feeling of coercion.

Further distinctions between types of traction may be possible but they are not needed for our purpose. There is, however, one

63

experience that is akin to traction, though not necessarily associated with specific characteristics of the job. That is the well-known observation that workers are stimulated in their effort by the knowledge that output is expanding and that there is a pressure of work. Similarly, rumours about shortage of orders are known to have a depressing effect on activity. The classical example is that of the mica splitting girls in the Hawthorne studies, whose output generally declined when the work schedules had to be reduced in view of the 1930 depression. Although the overall psychological effect of production is difficult to isolate as a separate factor in motivation, the similarity to traction effects helps us to understand such situations. Line traction in particular acts as a psychological multiplier of the external output situation. The operator feels himself as a particle in the ceaseless flow of activity. Any step towards increased flow production intensifies that feeling. Similarly, if there is in the factory an all-round atmosphere of speed and pressure of production, no one can escape being affected by it. The similarity between line traction and general production traction also follows from the fact that it makes little difference whether line production is based on mechanical conveyors or human chains, whereby the manufactured article passes through a consecutive series of operations by being handed on from one operator to the next.

I have described traction at some length, and with more emphasis than I gave to tedium, its counterpart, for a good reason. Traction is probably the most important, in any case the most specific, example in the industrial context of relative satisfactions. These are, as I mentioned before, feelings that arise as a relief from fundamentally disliked situations, and they are very difficult to understand.[1] The operator need not be conscious of the relativity of traction. It is quite possible that he usually, if not always, has the definite impression that traction is a genuine satisfaction inherent in particular operations. The

---

[1] As a matter of fact, in my first description of traction (Baldamus (1951a and b) I did not realize how much it was a kind of pseudo-satisfaction. But this has also been overlooked by all those who described, usually in chance observations, the same phenomenon under the name of 'rhythm', 'swing', 'momentum', 'pull', etc.

ordinary worker has few opportunities to compare experiences from widely differing occupations. If he is a semi-skilled repetition worker, he can compare only a limited range of similar operations, and therefore, taking it for granted that his job is bound to be fundamentally tedious, he will then strive to obtain a job where traction is relatively strong and interferences to traction small. He will also tend, normally, to take the external situation for granted: the need to have a dissatisfying job at all, the necessity to 'keep going', to follow the line of least resistance. Thus, only at the particular moment when there are special imperfections, irritations, and interferences with the usual type of traction, only then does he become aware, vaguely and reluctantly, of the deprivation fundamentally inherent in the work realities of tedium. In other words, traction (or any other relative satisfaction) tends to become a normal expectation; a feeling that is projected into the currently accepted definition of routine operations.

CHAPTER 7

Weariness and Contentment

A DESCRIPTION of work feelings is not complete unless it includes the phenomenon of 'fatigue'. It is often thought that this is a well-established technical term among industrial psychologists. Unfortunately, this is by no means the case. Ryan and Smith (1954, p. 288), summarize the situation thus: 'Important as it is in the total cost of work to the individual, the feeling of tiredness resulting from the work is extremely difficult to quantify and to reckon into the evaluation of human efficiency. . . . As more and more difficulties have turned up in dealing with the more 'objective' measures of fatigue, a new attack upon the problem of evaluating subjective fatigue would seem to be in order at the present time.' They suggest that subjective fatigue be associated with 'the feeling of the individual of being unpleasantly tired, unable to enjoy his evening of leisure, feeling discontented with a life which requires him to work until he develops these unpleasant feelings' (ibid. p. 288). This approach is similar to the attempt by Bartley and Chute (1947, p. 340) to separate fatigue, as an intangible state of mind, from impairment, which is directly determined by organic factors. A number of qualitative criteria are mentioned for instance: 'A peculiarly mobilized conflict exists between inclination and duty or external compulsion, and fatigue results'; 'An individual who has been relatively free from conflict during a prolonged period of physical activity is much less fatigued than an individual who faced numerous conflicts in the course of a similar activity' (ibid. p. 399). It should be noted that both Ryan and Smith and Bartley and Chute connect tiredness with the notion that an individual is 'required' or 'compelled' to work.

To carry this approach a little further, I shall use the term 'weariness' in a similar though more specific sense. This can be done, in the first place, by relating weariness to an awareness of the total situation characteristic of a job, a particular kind of employment or occupation. We are then concerned with being tired of the daily grind of work, employment or service as such, rather than with the technical details of industrial activities. Weariness is in this respect more akin to an attitude than is either impairment or tedium. This explains why it is so difficult to identify the corresponding work realities. If these can be located, however approximately, the concept will lose much of its vagueness.

Probably the most characteristic attribute of weariness is the apparently inexplicable suddenness with which it appears and disappears.[1] One feels suddenly depressed about the whole job situation, and yet is aware that the feeling will pass without one's doing anything about it. Significantly, this may be experienced independently of such conditions as induce impairment and tedium. This is undoubtedly a matter of perception: one defines the situation by emphasizing its unpleasant features in a general way, without being able to pinpoint any particular aspect.[2] There is, however, one symptom that appears to be fairly typical. This is an awareness of the coercive nature of the situation. It comes to light, for instance, in the remarkable emphasis that factory and office workers place on whether the time passes slowly or quickly. The compulsion to 'keep going' and to make the hours of work pass as quickly as possible seems to be uppermost in their minds whenever weariness becomes acute. The importance of 'time experience' was first recognized, through participant observation, by M. Jahoda who also noticed that it varies according to age: 'Another difference between the time experience of younger and older girls is that the former are concerned with the day only, while the latter think of the hours of boredom, of the same kind experienced in the past and the inescapable future. In such a mood they would say something

[1] Unless otherwise stated, the following is drawn from personal experience.

[2] A useful description of weariness (in office work) which strikingly shows its connection with the whole job situation may be found in an early novel by Sinclair Lewis, *The Job*.

67

like, "Day after day, year in year out, always the same" ' (Marie Jahoda (1941), p. 202). The universal incidence of this kind of time-oriented perception recurs with certain variations. The curious abruptness and impetus with which workers hurry off from work may be mentioned in particular (Georges Friedmann (1950), pp. 65ff). There is also the preoccupation with leisure, holidays, hobbies, or other opportunities that provide an escape, real or imagined, from the routine of coercive regularity.[1] One would therefore expect a worker's conception of weariness to be, in a sense, a function of his attitude to leisure. But leisure is probably also evaluated in its own right. With the secular trend towards shorter working-hours, the whole conception of leisure time tends to become articulate as an independent factor. Thus, as it would be very difficult to isolate, any attempt to use the evaluation of leisure as an index of weariness would seem unprofitable.

In the light of present knowledge, I suggest that the most plausible decisive work reality in weariness is the coercion inherent in the institution of industrial employment. The only assumption necessary is that coercive routines are universally disliked. If, in other words, the coercive regularity and continuity of employment are felt to be intolerable, it will be experienced as a painful discomfort in much the same way as the physical strain of heavy work and the tedium of highly repetitive activities. By 'degree of coercion' I mean, first of all, the number of working-hours considered necessary in given circumstances for a particular job or occupation; secondly, the way the total working-time is customarily divided by means of shifts, rest pauses, holidays, etc. Office routines, for instance, are in that sense less coercive than factory routines.

The capacity for enduring coercive routines will, of course, vary between different persons, but that also applies to impairment. It is obviously not necessary here to know where the exact threshold of tolerance to coercion lies. Nor do we need to know the nature of the corresponding physiological processes, if indeed there are any. I define weariness simply as a

[1] For a general discussion of this see David Riesman (1950).

state of mind in which the coerciveness of routine work is consciously unbearable or acutely unpleasant.

By stressing the total situation in contrast to specific methods of production, we are less likely to confuse weariness with tedium. There have been several recent studies that suggested that a feeling of coercion is also an important factor in highly repetitive work. 'The principal source of dissatisfaction stemmed', according to Charles Walker's inquiry into assembly work, 'from the machine pace and lack of individual control over this pace (C. H. Walker and R. H. Guest (1952), pp. 26f, 126ff.). It is significant here that this study started off with a different hypothesis; lack of meaning and low skill were at first expected to be the main causes of dissatisfaction. But the importance of coercion eventually emerged from the interviews as a separate factor. More or less the same thing seems to have happened in the course of an inquiry into repetitive work by David Cox *et al.* (1953, p. 26), who also came to recognize 'constraint' as of greater influence than originally expected. In both cases, the main focus was on tedium rather than weariness. It would anyway be difficult empirically to maintain a sharp distinction between the two. However, brief, infrequent periods of tedious activity are obviously possible without serious discomfort. The strain will become cumulative only when they occur day after day and week after week. It is then that the worker tends to project the coerciveness of the whole situation back into feelings experienced during the actual operation. Thus, his accumulated memories of the constraint to 'keep going' will become part of his customary definition of the situation. As tedium and weariness are difficult to separate in practice, it is all the more necessary to maintain an analytical distinction between the corresponding work realities of repetitiveness on the one hand, and the coercion of prolonged routine work on the other.

Since weariness has been defined as a special kind of deprivation, there should be a corresponding relative satisfaction. This would have to be a projection such as to make the strain of coercive routines tolerable. Workers are obviously not affected

69

all the time by the feeling of weariness caused by the awareness of coercion. As we have seen, weariness comes and goes abruptly. The feeling which replaces it by way of relief may be described as 'contentment', a state of mind that is often expressed by saying that one is in the mood for work. This is usually a kind of dull contentment, though it may be more positive in the case of marked susceptibility to weariness. The nature of contentment may best be understood by referring back to what I said with regard to psychological inurement, a condition connected with the physical environment of strenuous work. A contented working mood is in a way similar to inurement but differs in that its projective quality is more articulated. When the phrase 'one gets used to it' is applied to the coercion of routine work, as it frequently is, it implies much more of a deliberate resolution to resign oneself to inescapable necessities than is the case with inurement, which is simply a passive experience of the absence of bodily discomfort. It seems, therefore, that an act of will is required in order to get into the right working mood. That is to say, 'getting used' to coercion need not be entirely an automatic process dependent only on length of time. To some extent, disturbing and disliked but unavoidable conditions can be ignored by directing one's attention to other matters and so becoming resigned to the necessity of keeping one's job, or realizing that any other job would also involve the overall coercion of work routines. This process of active adjustment may therefore support, or even enhance, a state of mind already conditioned by inurement.

The relation between traction and contentment is similar to that between tedium and weariness. Just as the two deprivations are closely intertwined empirically, so are their counterparts of traction and contentment. The accumulated memories of traction elements can easily be projected, as contentment, into an overall attitude towards the job. It is well known that operations or jobs that are full of irritations and poor in traction are relatively disliked. One of the most common experiences, familiar to all who have had personal insight into industrial work, is the curious habit of tricking oneself into a pleasant working mood by first getting rid of all the more distracting and irritating operations so as to have a smooth run of traction-involving activities to look forward to. A telling illustration of this in the Hawthorne Experiments is the bankwirer's habit of doing the most awkward wiring connections first, so as to be able to do the rest in a smooth self-sustaining run. Similarly, workers who are prone to weariness in the afternoon tend to do the more unpleasant activities in the morning and save the operations with higher traction for the afternoon. All this shows how a deliberate adjustment may help to produce a state of contentment. And it also indicates the close interaction between traction and contentment.

It is therefore not surprising that in the relevant literature no clear distinction between the two phenomena has been drawn. Otherwise, however, it does support their existence. This is very evident in many descriptions of work curves. The most universal element of work curves, which is seldom if ever absent, is the initial rise of the daily output curve at the beginning of a day's work and again after the midday break. It reflects the gradual 'warming up' to a rapid and easy flow of activity, displacing weariness. The result of the warming-up phase has been called a state of being 'settled' at work.[1] This condition is one of the many indications of the working mood. It may also occur outside industrial employment if the conditions are similar. It is described, for example, by H. M. Vernon (1921, p. 82) in reference to the unpleasantly coercive task of marking a large batch of examination papers: 'I often experienced a feeling of irritation . . . when I first started work in the morning, but this soon wore off and was replaced by a feeling of apathy.' Occasionally it has also been observed that the ordinary learning process in industrial training often includes the acquisition of an attitude favourable to the smooth performance of the task, and the development of this attitudinal element may take much longer than the time necessary to master the actual operation (Cp.

[1] As these concepts are often used in the sense of technical terms, it should be noted that their origin is purely introspective. They were invented for the description of simple mental operations by E. Kraepelin (1902), p. 474, and adapted to industrial work by Max Weber (1908-09).

F

Wyatt, Fraser, and Stock (1929), pp. 37–8). Another link with past research may be seen in what has frequently been described as the worker's 'conservatism' in his preference for established habits and routines. This has been brought to light chiefly in field experiments to test the effects of a change in activities during the day, or spell, on attitudes and performance.[1] According to one of these studies, the fact that 'operatives accustomed to uniformity in the methods and conditions of work are reluctant to change to a more varied form of procedure, . . . is merely another illustration of the inertia produced by long-established habit and the desire to live along the lines of least resistance' (Wyatt, Fraser, and Stock (1928), p. 52). It is no contradiction that experiments with 'variety in work' have often been positive as regards contentment; the point is that the benefits of more varied work (i.e. a different type of work in mornings and afternoons) only appear after a period of adjustment: after the changeover itself, repeated once or twice a day, has become part of the habitual pattern which no longer interferes with the working mood.

It is difficult to say why the working mood results in contentment, except that it is felt as a relief.[2] Apparently it reduces the need to make an effort of will, especially the ever-present need to keep going along the path of minutely prescribed factory routines. Though it must be left to the professional psychologist to investigate the mental processes of this state of mind, a few external symptoms may be added by way of impressions and conjectures. I found, for example, that the sudden drying up of chatting and unrest in a face-to-face group of workers is a fairly typical indication of a working mood. At times, as though acting on a prearranged plan, everybody seems to withdraw into a phase of silent and absorbed activity, even though it may

---

[1] Cf. The *Journal of the National Institute of Industrial Psychology*, Vol. I (1921), p. 236; H. M. Vernon *et al.* (1924); Wyatt, Fraser, and Stock (1928); Cox *et al.* (1951); Charles Walker (1950).

[2] For the fullest description of work contentment compare P. Hall and H. W. Locke (1938). However, like many other studies on attitudes to work, this description takes any symptom of contentment at its face value and completely overlooks the role of substitute goals.

be meaningless repetition work. Another symptom, perhaps, is a comparatively smooth and steady output. Although a contented mood may unaccountably disappear and give rise to a sudden awareness of weariness, external conditions seem to have some effect. The ability to capture and maintain a working mood changes, for instance, according to the day of the week, Monday and Saturday apparently being the least conducive to it. The same applies to days immediately before and after holiday periods. It has long been known that output levels for such days are relatively low. A related fact is that Mondays (and to some extent Saturdays and after-holiday periods) are characterized by unusually high absence rates.

The problem deserves further attention for the following reasons. Though all behaviour indices are the result of simultaneously operating factors, this difficulty is comparatively less marked in the case of day-to-day variations in absence. By and large the work realities of a given situation (such as physical conditions, payment systems, type of supervision) do not change from day to day. Thus, if we find a consistent pattern in changes of the daily number of absentees within a week, the most likely cause must be sought in the worker's subjective definition of the situation. As a matter of fact, the observation that the number of absentees decreases from Monday to Friday in regular steps (see *Table 3*, p. 23 above), was unexpected because from a common-sense point of view one would imagine the opposite to happen.[1] It appeared, moreover, that in comparing different occupations, the decline in day-to-day absence in the course of a week tends to become less marked as the level of skill rises. One could think of many reasons to account for either the Monday or the Friday as exceptional days in the (five-day) working-week, but the real problem is to explain, not the exceptional character of one day, but the consistent change throughout the week. The emphasis, in view of this, must be put on variations in attitudes to work.

We might say, therefore, that there is a continuous process

[1] This is further discussed by Baldamus and Behrend (1950) and Behrend (1953), p. 71.

of adjustment during the week, resulting in a gradual improvement of the working mood, a process that is possibly supported by increasing inurement in the case of heavy work. It is thus the habitual working mood which breaks down, at least partly, with the disruption of the work routine by the weekend. Weariness is felt most acutely on Monday morning, and from then on the working mood is gradually recaptured as the week goes by, with only minor interruptions caused by the daily interference of home and leisure activities. That the steepness of the absence gradient decreases with higher levels of skill would mean that coercion, and therefore weariness, is relatively weaker according to occupational skill.

Undoubtedly all these observations on weariness and contentment should be received cautiously. The only way to clarify motivational concepts is to make our frame of reference more complex. I shall therefore suggest, though only in passing, one further type of deprivation which may be described as 'status deprivation'. It refers to the particular kind of dissatisfaction focused on the restrictions imposed by organizational status. The relevant work reality is the deprivation inherent in a given position, relative to any higher status level within the organization. The hostility towards positions of leadership in small groups and working teams is also pertinent here.

It can be seen at a glance that status sentiments are far more a matter of socially determined projections than any one of the other deprivations. A great deal of what seems to be status hostility is actually connected with type of work and level of skill; the envy for a higher status will often include aspects of work content, such as a lesser degree of physical strain, repetitiveness, and coercion. If these are analytically eliminated, what remains are specifically social and institutional factors, notably status barriers.

In so far as status deprivation may be considered as a separate sentiment, would it be possible to identify a relative satisfaction corresponding to it? Though it is difficult to define, there does seem to be a relevant projection. For lack of a better term, it may be called 'vindictiveness' towards persons of higher status.

74

The word is rather too strong, for it is intended to describe the peculiar satisfaction of 'getting one's own back'. It is a sentiment that can be observed in numerous shades and variations, and it is certainly a substitute goal. As a projected defence mechanism against frustrated status aspirations, vindictiveness is a problem for which an analysis in terms of human relations and group dynamics would be most suitable. But so far it has received little attention. The only study that, to my knowledge, has been clearly aware of it as a specific satisfaction is Jaques's (1951, pp. 85, 306ff., 312) description of the social atmosphere in works committees. The evidence suggests that all sorts of grievances are constantly nursed and perceptually elaborated because the concomitant feelings aroused in that way offer some relief from tensions and stresses that cannot be resolved effectively within the objective limitations of the external situation. Usually, and even in this investigation, references to substitute goals in connection with hostility are not very explicit. Such sentiments are anyway extremely intangible and therefore best treated as potential reinforcements to other, more tangible reactions.[1]

Above all it is probable that status frustrations are closely connected with coercive routines and so with weariness. Obviously, an important cause of coercion rests on status barriers. The compulsion of keeping a particular job is at least partly the result of being unable to move into a higher status position. Weariness may therefore often be the realization on the part of the employee that he has no chance of becoming an employer or of advancing to a managerial position. Thus, if we bear in mind that the deprivation inherent in the coercion of routine work contains a status factor, there is no need for us to extend the list of work realities and corresponding experiences. The further we move away from physically conditioned experiences (e.g. impairment) towards more complex sentiments such as status frustration, the more difficult it becomes to identify the

---

[1] For a remarkably vivid illustration see Donald Roy (1952): hostility comes to the surface only indirectly through symbols and expressive attitudes, superimposed upon the more solid basis of restrictive practices of withholding effort.

75

effective work realities. It will normally be sufficient to rely on the three most conspicuous work realities: physical working conditions, repetitiveness, and coercive routines. The typically corresponding deprivations are impairment, tedium, and weariness. These in turn are associated with three forms of relative satisfaction: inurement, traction, and contentment. This makes a list of nine criteria:

Work Realities	Physical Conditions	Repetitive-ness	Routines
Deprivations	Impairment	Tedium	Weariness
Relative Satisfactions	Inurement	Traction	Contentment

As we have seen, the connection between these groups is fairly simple: relative satisfactions are conditioned by deprivations and deprivations by work realities. Thus, a worker cannot experience relative satisfactions unless there are deprivations in work and there can be no deprivations unless there are specific work realities.

This is all that can be taken as reasonably well established. But of equal significance is the fact that throughout this inquiry it has become increasingly clear that the psychology of work is beset with far more uncertainties than is generally admitted. Not only are deterrents to work conventionally described in subjective, common-sense terms, but their tendency to be substituted and concealed by relative satisfactions is also overlooked. The latter point is important. For whatever else the role of relative satisfactions may be, they certainly have the effect of making work feelings, if taken as a whole, a phenomenon which is highly unstable. Unpredictably, tedium may change at any moment into traction, and weariness into contentment. What is more, it is the very nature of relative satisfactions that they are a dependent variable: any increase of irksomeness in the work realities tends to be balanced by increased satisfactions.

The instability of work feelings also puts the whole problem of work effort into a new perspective. As has been shown in Part I, conceptions of effort are logically indispensable to all systems of contractual controls. They influence, partly, the effectiveness of occupational and effort-stability controls, and they determine, wholly, the effectiveness of effort-intensity controls. Under all conditions, management's and the employee's notions of effort are common-sense terms which point to the psychological 'costs' of work. Or, as T. A. Ryan has put it, 'what interests the practical man is that a person who is "working hard", "who is exerting himself", or "taking pains" should be paid accordingly' (T. A. Ryan (1947), p. 97). In the light of the foregoing discussions we can say now that these expressions refer to specific deprivations such as impairment, tedium, and weariness. For theoretical purposes we may therefore define effort as the sum total of these deprivations. But this definition is of no use for practical application because it ignores the instability of work feelings. Nor does it explain how conceptions of effort may be projected into concrete job contents in connection with managerial effort controls.

So we have come to a new problem. We have found that the components of effort are essentially unpredictable, unstable, and beyond any form of measurement. And yet they form (as we know from Part I) the substance of contractual controls that are precise and definite. Somehow it must be possible to bridge the gap between these two aspects of industrial administration. Unless this can be done, the effectiveness of regulative controls remains inexplicable. They would be as unpredictable as seems the motivation on which they are based.

PART III

Industrial Institutionalization

CHAPTER 8

Work Obligations

THE CONTRAST between the precision of regulative controls and the vagueness of the underlying motivation is most clearly indicated by managerial effort-intensity controls (see Chapter 4). We may recall, for example, that the introduction of incentives, usually connected with time-and-motion study, requires accurate standards of the 'right' level of effort 'required' in a given industrial situation. If we take this in conjunction with the previous analysis of effort, it means that employers and employees must have definite conceptions of what is the right degree of impairment, tedium, and weariness. One factor that tends to make these work feelings so stable is that the terms 'right' and 'required' contain a moral element. We are to that extent concerned with normative conceptions, so from here on the problem is sociological rather than psychological.

Once the normative aspect of work deprivations is recognized, the curious effect of relative satisfactions, and hence the apparent instability of work motivation, become less puzzling. Let us suppose that workers feel (for reasons that have not yet been discovered) that they are under some moral obligation to accept a certain degree of deprivation connected with employment. Relative satisfactions will then be experienced as an unexpected relief from the pressure of those obligations. If it is a commonly shared assumption between all employees that work *has to be* tedious, then the experience of traction becomes possible and will be the more intensive the stronger the underlying obligation is. Such obligations, however, cannot be explained unless they are connected with a number of related observations that place them in a wider social context. One may consider them, to start with, as part of the social foundations of industrial society. That ethical conceptions of duty support the mechanism of market exchanges was clearly observed by Marx, repeatedly emphasized by Alfred Marshall, and finally elaborated by Weber into the familiar thesis about the effects of protestant ethics on the evolution of capitalism. Today the existence of 'social foundations', 'institutional frameworks', or 'value patterns', which somehow surround the system of market relations, has become a commonplace of social science. All this may be summarized under the concept of the *'social supports'* of industrial society. It would seem, then, that work obligations are nothing more than a special instance of social supports.

Such an interpretation requires a brief excursion into general theory. Over the past decade, the explanation of social relations has become increasingly sophisticated through the growing influence of the theory of socialization.[1] One important element in this theory is the assumption that social interaction is 'structured' by basic attitudes (in the sense of moral standards of behaviour). These are acquired and shaped in the process of socialization, primarily (but not only) during the early stages of child development. The result is that specific role-expectations in the form of mutual obligations determine social behaviour. The particular advantage of this approach lies in its emphasis on values and norms that may be shared by different persons and thus produce a measure of stability in a given system of human interaction. For a time the theory remained restricted largely to the narrow range of face-to-face relations and it seemed difficult to extend its applications to institutions of greater complexity than primary groups. For example, the entire realm of industrial institutions appeared to be left out, a realm where formal regulations rather than moral standards, routine behaviour rather than spontaneous decisions, determine directly both social stability and social conflict. At most, it was possible to argue that the effectiveness of formal controls and bureaucratic routines is ultimately subject to certain limitations that stem from a remote background of moral principles

---

[1] M. Sherif (1936); Talcott Parsons (1951); Talcott Parsons, Robert F. Bales, and Edward A. Shils (1953); Talcott Parsons and Robert F. Bales (1955).

related, somehow, to work, effort, productivity, efficiency, investment, saving, income distribution, and so on. This argument has recently been followed up to such an extent that a great deal of the premises underlying modern economic theory have been re-interpreted along the lines of Parsonian concepts (Talcott Parsons and Neil J. Smelser, 1957). So far as it goes, the outcome is simply that even the most complex economic (including industrial) institutions reflect an environment of normative standards that are internalized through primary socialization in the family. However, there can be no doubt that this background of basic attitudes still remains merely a background. It conditions, but does not determine, economic decisions. It is capable of *supporting* a particular institution, but it does not with any precision *control* the specific activities within the institution. Normative attitudes are, in other words, merely a form of social *supports*.[1] If, for instance, people universally believe that work is a moral obligation such beliefs make the use of regulative controls—indirectly—more effective. This, however, is very different from the kind of normative standards that are related to effort and efficiency: these, as we shall see, have a direct and compelling effect as a mechanism of *control*.

The difference between supports and controls may be further characterized if the former are associated with primary and the latter with secondary socialization. It is customary to consider 'primary' socialization as that which refers to the internalization of basic attitudes by the child in the nuclear family, and 'secondary' socialization as concerned with later processes affecting the adult's personality (e.g. the acquisition of occupational standards of behaviour). Possibly the psychological

[1] One would therefore expect that a sociological analysis of economic institutions that relies on social supports remains vague and ineffective when it tries to include the more intricate process of economic transactions. If Parsons and Smelser's work nevertheless obtains a remarkable degree of precision, it should be noticed that this is by no means due to a more refined version of the earlier theory of socialization. What in fact happened was that, along with the earlier theory, an entirely different theory was introduced to make possible the construction of a precise model of economic actions. It is based on the concept of social 'exchange' —alleged to be identical with the older concept of 'interaction'. For a detailed critique see W. Baldamus (1957a).

83

processes by which attitudes or beliefs are incorporated into the personality are similar. There is also 'institutionalization' in both cases, in so far as the processes have a stabilizing effect on the institutions in question, the family in the first place, and occupation, employment, etc. in the second. However, such an approach is apt to conceal the differences. In particular, it is generally overlooked that primary socialization equips the individual with the basic values that remain highly indeterminate if it comes to the explanation of concrete decisions: they remain ethical 'principles' and do not articulate into specific standards of behaviour outside the institution of the family. The orientations, on the other hand, which we acquire in later life as members of occupational, political, and religious institutions are specific and relatively precise for the control of behaviour *within* these institutions. It is, therefore, preferable to use the concept of '*institutional controls*' in this context (cp. Schema, p. 12).

Returning to the institution of industrial employment, we have three elements to cope with. All activities are subject (i) to the remote and indirect influence of basic values originating as social supports in the process of (primary) socialization; (ii) to the more definite effect of institutional controls that are acquired in the course of employment itself; (iii) to the still more precise determination of behaviour from formal controls (cp. Schema, p. 12). The interplay of these forces may readily be illustrated by the situation that faces a young person on his first entry into industrial employment. He brings with him a set of general role-expectations of what is right and wrong for him as a wage-earner. If he comes from a working-class family he will probably define work as a necessary evil and may search for an opportunity where it is relatively 'easy' to obtain a fair amount of money. This expectation acts as a social support to the institution of employment. Then he will soon have to learn the established rules of restricting output or the acceptable standards of effort, and in due course he thus incorporates into his habitual pattern of behaviour a specific set of institutional controls. In addition, his activities are minutely prescribed by
84

the system of regulative controls that govern his particular job, the methods of production, the type of supervision, and the mode of wage-payment. The corresponding situation that faces the employer or the managerial executive in the early stages of his career is formally the same, though, of course, the content of the three factors is different.

The empirical problems presented by the effects of social supports are quite formidable. The moral obligation to work is so widely taken for granted, and at the same time takes so many different forms according to occupational status, that it becomes a very elusive matter for observation. One way of approaching it is to seek out those 'marginal' groups which do not, or only imperfectly, conform to the general values prescribed by our society. The case of tramps, drug addicts, and 'problem families' provides some insight into the motivation of those who are persistently unemployable. But even in these cases it often occurs that people who refuse to work nevertheless express some degree of conformity to approved standards of behaviour.[1] Further evidence about the effects of primary socialization on basic attitudes towards work and employment has come from a number of studies that show that class-origin has a determining influence in that respect. It appears from this that people with middle-class background (usually assessed in terms of the father's occupation) place relatively more emphasis on 'hard work' as a means of occupational success than those who come from a working-class family.[2] Little is known, however, of how moral attitudes towards work affect an employee's conception of effort in the context of his job situation.

An inquiry into this problem, based on interviewing, would have to rely on hypothetical questions so that, as far as possible, the influence of normative factors could be kept separate from the influence of external controls. To this end the following observations were obtained as a response to the key question: 'You probably do certain things in your job not actually

[1] For an empirical study of this see W. Baldamus and Noel Timms (1955); Noel Timms (1956).

[2] Cf. Richard Centers (1948); Elizabeth L. Lyman (1955), pp. 138ff.; and notably Herbert H. Hyman (1953), pp. 426ff.

specified in your contract. Suppose you are justifiably dissatisfied but can do nothing about your grievance short of finding another job. Would you, in the meantime, drop the extras?"[1] It should be noticed that the question is so formulated that an affirmative answer to it would be entirely legitimate even for people particularly sensitive to occupational obligations. The results may be condensed into three main points.

1. It was originally expected, on common-sense grounds, that moral obligations towards work would become increasingly powerful as one goes up the scale of occupational status. With rising income, therefore, the number of negative answers to the above question would tend to increase. This is roughly borne out by the actual results (as far as reliable income data could be obtained). 73 per cent of those earning less than £500 p.a. gave negative answers while the percentage of negative answers in the group earning over £800 p.a. was 81 per cent. In the central income group, £500–£800 p.a., the negative answers amounted to 75 per cent. The number of respondents in the three groups were: 131 less than £500, 95 from £500 to £800 and 42 over £800 p.a.

2. The effect of social origin on effort conceptions came out fairly clearly. The respondents were analysed into three approximately equal groups according to type of occupation and family background (i.e. father's occupation): (a) manual workers with working-class background, (b) white-collar workers with working-class background, and (c) white-collar workers with middle-class background. The second two groups included professional and self-employed people. Of all those who answered with an unqualified 'yes' to the main question,

[1] I am greatly indebted to Mrs. Eva M. Pritchatt who conducted this investigation. It comprised a random sample of 400 interviews (including a pilot study of 100 preliminary interviews) carried out mostly in the homes of the respondents. The interviewers were instructed to adapt the key question as far as necessary to the particular job situation of each respondent. Otherwise information concerning family background, training, income, job history and other personal data was obtained by means of a set questionnaire. The range of occupational status, measured chiefly in terms of earned income, extended from the lowest ranks of manual labour to professional people up to the level of university professors.

86

42 per cent belonged to the first group, 34 per cent to the second, and 24 per cent to the third group. (These results are significant at the 5 per cent level.)

3. As the figures quoted under point (1) suggest, the majority of respondents denied that they would reduce effort or, at any rate, gave an evasive answer.[1] In other words, a fundamental sense of duty appears to assert itself so strongly that it tends to override both the influence of class origin and the effects of occupational status. This particular result of the survey is not adequately assessable in terms of figures. The fact that the question aroused some degree of emotional response is in itself quite relevant to the problem. The whole complex of obligations to work appeared to be surrounded by feelings of guilt, a variety of rationalizations, and, often, a marked reluctance to articulate these attitudes into definite statements. It is also interesting, in that connection, that employers almost invariably refused permission to carry out the interviews at the place of employment. Few seemed to realize that a refusal to be drawn into the question comes very close to a negative answer to it. The inventiveness displayed in finding reasons for not reducing effort under the conditions prescribed by the question is also significant. Many said that in their particular job slacking off would have no effect anyway. Others pointed out that they enjoyed their work and would not therefore want to slack off— they were not conscious of any special effort or of doing 'any extras'. Finally, as many as 25 per cent of all the negative answers expressed a decidedly moralizing attitude. This may be illustrated by the following few examples: 'One is paid to do the job, therefore one does it; if I were the employer, I would expect the same.' 'I don't believe in scamping. One shouldn't slack off.' 'It is not fair to the others.' 'If you can't take enough interest in the job, you ought to give it up.'

Taking the evidence as a whole, we may conclude that attitudes towards work undoubtedly contain a normative element. Though partly affected by differences in occupational status and

[1] For further details cp. W. B. Baldamus (1960) chap. II.

G

social origin, work obligations are effective over a wide range of varying conditions. Being a product of socialization, they are a powerful and yet widely diffused determinant.

We have described work obligations at some length because they have been unduly neglected, compared with certain other social supports of industrial society that have attracted more attention, e.g. social standards of consumption, religious and political value systems, status aspirations. Among these supports is one that is nearly as closely connected with effort expectations as are work obligations: the cultural imperative of social ambition, in particular, the 'tradition of opportunity' in respect of upward social mobility. The significance of this factor to the present context is fairly obvious. It is also well documented by recent studies (C. Wright Mills, 1951; E. Chinoy, 1955). What has yet to be done is to follow up the impact of industrial social supports on related institutional controls.

CHAPTER 9

Standards of Effort Value

MORAL obligations which are formed during the early processes of socialization are an indispensable factor providing
some measure of organization in human behaviour. They have,
nevertheless, a serious defect in that function: however powerful, their content is too diffuse to control behaviour effectively
in any concrete situation. Institutional controls, derived from
secondary socialization, are much more specific and therefore a
more determinate force. As far as industrial activities are concerned, the most relevant type of institutional controls are
standardized conceptions of effort. In industry, they take the
form of what are variously called 'production standards', 'job-
values', 'work loads', 'standards of application', and 'standards
of effort'. These conceptions are always associated with normative attributes, such as 'required', 'normal', 'fair', 'right', and
so on.[1] This indicates that they are founded on generalized
obligations to work; what remains to be explained is the process
that makes them specifically defined standards of behaviour.

To appreciate the importance of institutional controls in
industry, the instability of work motivation, and particularly
the vagueness of current notions of effort and labour efficiency,
has to be borne in mind throughout the following discussion.
If, indeed, effort conceptions are a form of institutional control,
one would expect them to be part of the employment contract.
To see this, the contract should be associated with the concept
of the firm in the widest sense, consisting of an employer to
whom an employee surrenders a certain amount of effort in
return for wages. For a less abstract approach, the specific

[1] This has been most extensively documented by Van Dusen Kennedy (1945).
Cp. also F. Fürstenberg (1955).

relations between first-line supervisors and operatives on the shop-floor level may be taken as an alternative. That these particular relations are in fact the pivot on which industrial organization revolves even in its most complex development has been increasingly recognized in recent years, see, for example, G. D. H. Cole (1957), pp. 38f, 56ff. The content of the employment contract would seem very obvious from this vantage point: it should express the amount of wages that have to be paid for certain amounts of effort of a given type. But the moment we argue on such grounds and then look at the facts, a most extraordinary thing reveals itself. However elaborate it may be, the contract does not do this. Though it stipulates precise wage payments for the employer, nothing definite is ever said about effort or efficiency; nor anything about the components of effort, the acceptable intensity of impairment, the tolerable degree of tedium or weariness. Instead it merely mentions hours of work, type of job, occupational status, and similar external conditions. At the most, there are vague and concealed references to an implied level of effort. A comparatively detailed contract may be quoted by way of illustration: a collective agreement between the Federated Associations of Boot and Shoe Manufacturers and the National Union of Boot and Shoe Operatives (January 1954) requires from the employer to 'pay the full rates of wages for all output', and from the employees, 'to use their trade skill and productive ability to the best advantage and fullest capacity and with no restriction of output following a change of organization or machinery'. But who can define ability, restricted output, capacity ('fullest' or otherwise)? If the intensity of effort expected from the worker is undefined, then, surely, everything else that is stated about wages, hours, and method of payment is equally indeterminate. For it is hardly logical to say that a man is paid so-and-so much per hour or per piece in a particular job unless it is also explained precisely how hard he should work at it. Thus the formal contract between employer and employee is *incomplete* in a very fundamental sense.

Although this gap should be evident even to the casual

observer, it is very rarely admitted. The following statement by Herbert A. Simon is the only recognition of it which I have come across: 'To an employee of a non-volunteer organization, the most obvious personal incentive that the organization has to offer is a salary or wage. It is a peculiar and important characteristic of his relation with the organization that, in return for this inducement, he offers the organization not a specific service but his undifferentiated time and effort (Herbert A. Simon (1946), pp. 115–16). In trying to explain this, Simon goes on to ask: 'How can this be? Why does the employee sign a blank cheque, so to speak, in entering upon his employment?' Two reasons are given: (i) Nothing would be gained, from the viewpoint of the organization, without the employee's 'acceptance of its authority'. (ii) As regards the employee, 'the precise activities with which his time of employment is occupied may, within certain limits, be a matter of relative indifference to him'. Such an explanation, however, is manifestly inadequate. The second point does little more than beg the question, for we are still not told *why*, and within *what* limits, the worker is indifferent to signing a blank cheque. As a matter of fact, we shall later see that the degree of acceptable exertion is of the utmost importance to him.

The true reason for the indeterminate employment contract is that it could not possibly be complete, on purely logical grounds. This follows from our analysis of work motivation. From this we know that the employee's effort is tantamount to deprivations, and deprivations are work feelings that are essentially unstable. For example, a formally complete agreement would have to take into account not only the irksomeness of work, but also the relative satisfactions; there would have to be a highly subjective description for every type of work and for all working conditions. Evidently, some sort of summarily standardized expectations of effort are indispensable. As a first approximation, such standards may be understood as a means of defining tacitly the obligation to work at a certain level of effort. Most characteristic are standards of behaviour that are related to what is called 'restriction of output'. Although the

91

term permits various interpretations, it clearly points to tacit agreements on the level of effort thought to be required in a given situation.

Inquiries into restriction of output have therefore provided most of what we know at present about effort standards that support the employment contract and make it workable. First of all, there are the familiar 'rules' of the bankwirers discovered in the Hawthorne Experiments ('you must not be a rate-buster'; 'you must not be a chiseler', etc.). They have often been quoted as a striking illustration of informal groups among workers. But though this aspect is certainly important, the emphasis that has been put on it has, unfortunately, overshadowed the wider significance of output standards as an indispensable element in agreements between management and workers. The same applies to an inquiry by Donald Roy that is otherwise most remarkable for its penetrating insights obtained through participant observation.[1] Here at last we have a sharply articulated situation defined in terms of standardized effort. It is a machine shop under piecework conditions, and restriction of output is thoroughly established. Two conceptions are predominant in the workers' minds: 'stinkers' and 'gravy jobs'. They refer, respectively, to jobs on which it is either very difficult or very easy to make a reasonable amount of money. 'On "gravy jobs" the operators earned a quota, then knocked off. On "stinkers" they put forth only minimal effort; either they did not try to achieve a turn-in equal to the basic wage rate or they deliberately slowed down' (op. cit. p. 436). To anyone who reads Roy's report carefully, the most conspicuous point is the high degree of certainty with which different kinds of operation are compared and summarily classified as 'bad' or 'good', 'hard' or 'easy'. This does not only imply that different people must experience the various components of effort in a similar way. It also means that they share specific expectations in respect of gross earnings; for the criteria of 'good' and 'bad' refer to the

---

[1] Donald Roy (1952). The results of Roy's study have been strongly confirmed by a similar investigation by the Department of Social Anthropology at Manchester University: cf. Tom Lupton and Sheila Cunnison (1957).

varying chances of earning a given amount of money. Thus, what is standardized is in fact the *value* of effort in terms of the employee's wage expectations.

A particularly significant contribution of Roy's inquiry is the distinction of two major types of restriction of output: 'quota-restriction' and 'goldbricking', according to whether the effort values are conceived as generous or stingy. There is a third type, the 'slowdown', which is simply a more serious form of goldbricking arising from extremely 'tight' piece rates. It is of special interest to any analysis of industrial conflict that quota-restriction and ordinary goldbricking do not necessarily result in open conflict. Manifest hostility is, however, clearly observable when the effort values are so unsatisfactory (from the employee's standpoint) that goldbricking changes over into a deliberate slowdown, amounting to a form of sabotage. A brief glance at this situation, described as the 'hinge-base fight' (op. cit. pp. 437–8), may help to bring the crucial aspects of effort values into clearer perspective. The rate paid for certain drilling operations was considered to be extremely tight. During a prolonged struggle the rate increased gradually from 23 to 31 cents per piece, which was still judged as unsatisfactory by the operators. Throughout this time they exercised a pressure on management by ostensibly working far below their capacity. The time-study men, taking the employer's point of view, argued that the rate could not be raised further because the hinge-base was part of a jack of which the market price, though already unprofitably low, was still not competitive. It was suggested, in other words, that the rate has to remain tight because it would be only fair that the workers should share in the losses resulting from the low market price of the product. Needless to say, the argument was not accepted. We have here, therefore, a case illustrating very concisely an unusually complex matter, namely that effort values have a direct bearing on the distribution of productivity shares between management and workers. We shall return to this point in the next chapter.

The investigations of Lupton and Cunnison (op. cit) have thrown further light on the remarkably precise and rational

93

conceptions among operatives in respect of effort values. In particular, it was found that the intensity of effort required by a given operation varies frequently according to circumstances over which the worker has no control, such, as for instance, the continuity of supply of materials and components; his earnings would therefore fluctuate even though the rate for the job remained unchanged. Thus, on one and the same job the effort value would go up and down as a consequence of those circumstances. To counterbalance these potential fluctuations, the workers apply ingenious devices of overbooking and underbooking, or 'fiddling'. When the effort value appears high, the hours worked on the job, or the pieces produced, are underbooked so that there is a 'reserve' that may be called upon at a time when effort values are low. Such practices tend to be condoned by management, presumably because their effect is ultimately to prevent unnecessary variations in gross earnings. The upshot is, again, that all this can only be possible on the basis of stable and definite effort and wage expectations.

Considering that employees have ample opportunities as well as good reasons for exchanging and comparing experiences on different jobs, their aptitude for standardized conceptions of effort and wages is perhaps not surprising. But if these notions are to be effective in supplementing the employment contract, management would have to take them into account so that informal agreements, supporting the formal contract, become possible. That this is indeed the case is to some extent indicated by the principles underlying time-and-motion study, and rate-setting generally. It is fairly well known that preconceived notions about 'required' standards of effort, output, skill, and rates of work are indispensable to efficient administration. To quote from the most representative textbook on time-study (italics mine): The aim of time-study is to 'determine by scientific measurement the number of standard hours in which an average man can do the job' (op. cit. p. 8). 'In order to set *equitable* time standards for doing any task, it is necessary to establish certain criteria of performance. To this end, a *normal reasonable* performance called the average performance has

94

been arbitrarily established by definition. It is the performance given by the operator who works with *average* effort. . .' (Lowry, Maynard, & Stegemerten (1940), p. 9). This concept is further discussed as follows: 'The useful range (of effort) is divided into six general classifications: poor, fair, average, good, excellent, and excessive (pp. 216–17). . . 'The average effort falls on the border line between the *fair* and the *good* effort. It is the effort to which all others are compared, and yet it is perhaps the hardest to define specifically. . . The operator exerting the average effort works steadily and with *fairly good* system. He will not deny that he is not doing his *best*, but he feels justified in holding back because he somewhat doubts the *fairness* of time-study or of the time-study man' (p. 221).

If we compare these evaluations of effort with those expressed by the operators, they are very similar in so far as, again, a process of standardization reveals itself in terms of purely moral judgements. However, the practical significance of these conceptions cannot be taken for granted merely on the basis of a general textbook. The following statements, obtained from a survey on incentives and methods of rate-setting,[1] provide some evidence that they *are* important. The statements illustrate typical answers to two questions: (i) 'How important do you consider the following difficulties in establishing accurate standard times as a basis for payment by results: to isolate external influences on performance, to determine average skill, to establish proper fatigue allowances, or other difficulties?' (ii) 'Do you know cases of loose or tight rates? Are they tolerated? If so, why?' Since all the firms interviewed were using either time-study or rate-fixing extensively, it was not to be expected that they would freely admit the subjective nature of these methods. In fact, there was always a varying degree of resistance to overcome, but despite this, the answers to the question show, on analysis, a very consistent and rather remarkable pattern. A few examples may be selected at random.

[1] For a full account of this survey see H. Behrend (1957) and W. Baldamus (1957b). It is based on a series of interviews with some forty-five representatives of management and fifteen trade union officers, covering firms of a wide range of different sizes and methods of wage payment.

One respondent admitted that the determination of average effort and average skill is difficult. 'But if the supervision is good and practical, they can estimate from experience'. In reply to the second question, he said, 'Tight rates do not last for long, loose rates do. They can only be adjusted by negotiation, and are difficult to adjust down because of union strength. Sometimes the job method has to be changed.'

Another respondent said that the isolation of external influences and the determination of average effort, average skill, and proper fatigue allowances are all important difficulties. When rates have been set, an 'efficiency study' is carried out periodically and the planning department is told of any abnormally high earnings. 'They would not take any action to tighten such a rate, but would bear it in mind when further timing was to be done. When very loose or tight rates have been set, advantage is taken of a reciprocal agreement (regarding adjustments) between management and Trade Unions: both sides see the value of a reasonable attitude.'

In one case we were told, 'The determination of average effort has to be a subjective decision. If rates are set tight, there is an implied right of appeal through shop stewards. If rates are set loose it is a matter of good will. A watch is kept over the level of earnings by shops and individuals. Methods of production may be changed, but the firm takes the view that it has no legal right to cut the rate. If a man is unreasonable, the union may be brought in'.

In another case, the first question was not applicable because a crude form of rate-fixing was used instead of time-study, but in answer to the second question we were told: 'Always, of course, workers object to a new rate as too tight: then the rate-fixer takes off his coat and demonstrates that it *can* be done. If rates are loose, management sticks to its bad bargain until method change becomes possible. There is a continuous process of rate adjustment and even bargaining between rate-fixers and workers'.

On one occasion the respondent said that none of the difficulties was important. There were no real difficulties. The

96

determination of average effort might require a good deal of practice, but it was all merely a question of training. One department had complained of tight rates; the union had agreed to calling in and half paying for an outside consultant. He confirmed the management's timing and the workers then accepted the standards. On the whole, loose rates are not adjusted once the rate has been fixed; one cannot do anything about it unless the job is changed.

Similarly, 'We do have tight rates, but they are not tolerated by the company or the employees. Disagreement on rates is first of all argued out between time-study man and operator: if no agreement can be reached, the foreman may be called in, then the shop steward. The matter may be taken to management level, but rarely is. Normally, loose rates are only adjusted by method change and subsequent negotiation.'

These are answers from management interviews. Although there are differences of opinion about the difficulties connected with rate-setting, the existence of standardized expectations about effort and wages is clearly expressed. A few examples from answers by trade union representatives to the second question may serve to strengthen the point.

'If a rate becomes tight because the job is done on a different machine or with different material, we would demand a re-rating or an allowance; loose rates are not usually altered unless they are quite silly and in such a case the worker should tell the rate-fixer that he would take less for the job, to forestall re-rating or method change.'

'An experienced worker knows how many pieces he can do in a day, and therefore knows what price he should get. A newcomer should ask a fellow worker with longer service what he thinks the job is worth and use this estimate in his bargaining with the rate-fixer.'

'Tight rates are very difficult to get altered; the best way is to find a loose job and a tight job and agree to have them both re-rated, because then it works both ways. Recently a group of men agreed to pay back money they had been paid through mistiming; this amounted to £1 18*s*. 9*d*. for each worker. A

97

week or two previously these men had been on a tight rate and the management had given them 14*s*. each to make up for it.'

Taken as a whole, the interviews leave no doubt that standards of effort value are a significant element in the attitudes of both managers and union representatives. Moreover, if these observations are taken in conjunction with the evidence from several inquiries on workers' behaviour mentioned earlier, such conceptions appear to be a decisive factor throughout the pattern of industrial relations on the shop-floor level.

Although it is true that all the evidence has come solely from piecework, it should not be overlooked that the concept of effort value applies to time rates in exactly the same way. This follows already from the fact that effort and wages are a necessary and general component of the employment contract under any conditions whatsoever. So even under daywork, unless there is some tacit reference to prevailing effort values, the contract would not be workable. Hence the notion of 'loose' and 'tight' rates makes sense also when wages are paid by the hour. The only difference is that with piecework the relevant expectations become more accentuated and thus more conscious to the participants in the situation. We are, therefore, entitled henceforth to treat the concept of effort value as a tool of analysis that has general applicability, independent of the method of wage payment.

But if on logical grounds the difference between piecework and daywork is negligible, it deserves some attention for other reasons. For as soon as one has recognized the general importance of effort values, the question arises: if this is true, why has it not been seen before? At least part of the answer points to the fact that current thinking on wages and wage policy tends to generalize from daywork conditions where effort conceptions are less precise and less conscious (particularly to the outsider). Furthermore, any agreement or bargaining about the right relationship between effort and pay is, with daywork, more difficult to visualize, since it is then concealed beneath the technicalities of administrative controls. The most usual approach is to dismiss such problems under the heading of

98

employee 'discipline'—without realizing that variations in discipline necessarily imply the existence of effort expectations.

Irrespective of the methods of wage payment, two general conclusions may be drawn from the available observations. First, all judgements on effort values are a combination of effort and wage expectations: the evaluation of the right effort is inseparately fused into judgements on appropriate earnings. The result is that effort standards become, through this link with wages, more precise than they otherwise could be. Second, both management and workers are more certain in recognizing the wrong relation of effort to wages than the correct one: the various processes of adjustment (job-bargaining, job rotation, fiddling, rate-cutting, re-timing, quota-restriction, goldbricking, etc.) are focused on effort values that are (from the worker's standpoint) too high or too low. In other words, there is a margin within which job values may move up or down without provoking definite judgements and corrective adjustments.

If this is taken into account the remarkable degree of certainty attached to standardized expectations of effort is no longer surprising. For it means that rigidly institutionalized notions of upper and lower limits can be effective even if there is some latitude (and uncertainty) around the intermediate effort values between those limits. Obviously, under conditions that have remained comparatively stable over long periods, the margin will be smaller and more tangible than in a changing situation. A stable situation greatly facilitates judgements on effort because it demands relative rather than absolute conceptions; a particular level of effort can be assessed as wrong, without specifying the components of effort, simply by comparing it with the customary conditions already prevailing in the job situation. And if very similar operations have to be compared, it will suffice to consider differences in those aspects only that are characteristic of the type of operation, as perhaps the degree of tedium or a special form of irksomeness. In the worker's definition of the situation, minute details are often very important for his evaluation of customary effort levels (compare

99

in this context the discussion on traction and tedium in Chapter 6. pp. 60–64).

In all this, we should notice, it is always the employee's experience in which the process of institutionalization is rooted. It appears to be the ultimate authority as far as effort values in a stable situation are concerned. The employer, the supervisor, or the time-study man can do no more than estimate, usually with the help of measurements of performance, the marginal effort standards that originate in the mind of the wage-earner. This is indeed the reason why the routines of successful rate-fixing and job-evaluation require a great deal of practical experience and close familiarity with the physical and psychological conditions of the job situation, as is always emphasized in textbooks and manuals on work measurement. It is also the explanation for the fact that wide discrepancies in the rating of effort among different practitioners occur when the rating is done under unfamiliar conditions artificially created for experimental purposes (see W. Rodgers and F. M. Hammersley, 1954). Moreover, as has been shown in Chapter 3, the use of effort-stability controls is not possible without at least rudimentary conceptions of effort; if seen in an environment of firmly institutionalized expectations of effort value, their effectiveness in controlling stability of performance can leave no doubt. Provided that the external market conditions are sufficiently enduring to preclude major organizational changes, institutional controls are capable of projecting an element of predictability into the whole range of administrative techniques, ranging from simple supervision to the most complex methods of automatic production. Finally, to recall one other problem that had to be left open at the beginning of this study: the astonishing degree of certainty that pervades all notions of 'efficiency' despite the lack of any reliable definition of the term. We now know that the only thing that really matters in any judgement on 'efficiency' is a judgement on 'effort', which in turn refers to the secure basis of established effort values.

The accent of the present chapter has been on effort rather than wages. It should not be overlooked, however, that the stability of effort values is partly also a function of institutionalized wage expectations. To consider this factor would lead us far afield and is in any case not required for the main trend of our analysis. As far as the bare facts go, there is sufficient evidence from other fields of inquiry that wage goals under stationary conditions are fairly rigid for a given job situation. Similarly to standards of effort, the relevant point is again the existence of a set margin of upper and lower limits for the adjustment of minor fluctuations. The most conspicuous, though not the only, stabilizing influence on wage expectations comes from institutionalized attitudes on the spending and saving of income determined by the prevailing culture of family life, leisure activities, peer groups, status aspirations, and the like.[1] In addition, another equally familiar factor may be mentioned in passing: the downward inflexibility of wages, which is largely a product of institutionalized trade-union goals. Nothing seems to be known, however, about the impact of trade unionism on the relation between wage and effort expectations.

As is usual, empirical findings advance our understanding in one direction but lead to new questions in another. A new problem poses itself if we return to the employment contract. Although the contract is now determinate, because we can argue that it commits the employee to a preconceived value of effort, this conclusion is limited to whatever happens to be customary under the institutional conditions of the time and the place to which the agreement refers. The question is therefore, how is it possible to define the commitment to certain effort values when market conditions fluctuate, when new methods of production are introduced, or when the supply of labour changes?

[1] Among numerous studies on the subject, H. Pipping (1953) is most relevant to the present context.

CHAPTER 10

Marginal Wage Disparity

SINCE almost everything about industrial institutionalization points towards rigidity, particularly in the light of typically large-scale organizations, the problem of adjustments to *changing* situations deserves special attention. In taking up this point, we intend the discussion that follows to supplement the analysis of effort-intensity controls outlined in Chapter 4. Part of the answer is very simple. As individual expectations vary with different persons according to social background, age, sex, and temperament, a firm may alter the average pattern of effort values by changing the composition of its labour force. This is possible even at relatively high levels of employment: by offering exceptionally high wages, well above the 'going rate', a firm puts itself into a position to attract a type of exceptionally 'efficient' worker.[1]

There is, however, another form of flexibility that is both more important and more problematic. It is achieved by changing the two components of effort value (that is to say: effort intensity and wages) in such a manner that the resultant value of effort remains *constant*. Theoretically, this amounts to movements in effort and wage expectations that are parallel. Suppose, for instance, that in a given firm a characteristically low level of wages is balanced by low standards of effort, as described by Gouldner (1955, pp. 31ff.) under the concept of an 'indulgency pattern'; now, if through some form of re-organization both components move upwards to the same extent, we obtain the opposite case of what might be called the 'stringency pattern', a

---

[1] The evidence available is scanty but sufficient for the present purpose; see K. G. J. C. Knowles (1951), M. Derber (1955), pp. 55f., 100f.; F. Fürstenberg (1958), p. 16.

situation with high earnings geared to a correspondingly higher level of effort intensity. Providing the movements are strictly parallel, the value of a unit of effort is in both cases the same. It has remained too low, too high, or adequate as the case may be. An analysis of the dynamics of industrial change, therefore, demands not only an examination of variations in effort value as such, but also of changes in the overall *level* of effort and pay expectations.

The unfamiliarity of this concept, and the difficulty of getting used to it, can best be overcome by envisaging its practical importance. It is no exaggeration to say that the whole history of industrial development persistently reveals adjustments around the contrast between indulgency and stringency patterns. The broad secular trend has undoubtedly been towards gradually increasing stringency. That is to say, while wages (nominal and real) have tended to increase, by and large the level of average effort intensity has also gone up, so that effort values in fact may have remained constant or have changed comparatively little. The process of secularly rising levels of effort intensity is at times concealed by concomitant reductions in hours of work. It should be noted that the components of effort may change without necessarily affecting overall effort intensity. Though, for example, one component, physical impairment, has gradually declined, others, like tedium and weariness, have grown in importance. In modern industry, two different versions of the stringency pattern are particularly interesting. One is that major advances in speeding up output through methods of automatic production have usually been achieved by simultaneous increases in pay, as is best known from the history of the Ford motor company. When wages are exceptionally high, often in addition to other benefits, a firm has the advantage of keeping a tight control over output and discipline because it can use the threat of dismissal more effectively. The second version of the same policy is the transition from day rates to payment by results such as piecework, bonus systems, and profit-sharing.

But the broad panorama of these trends does not show the strategic points of industrial change. A number of details

H

demand further attention. One aspect that has to be stressed is the fact that movements towards higher levels of wages and effort must unavoidably uproot the prevailing institutionalized standards of effort. Indeed, this is precisely the function of the concomitant rises in wages. Every step along the path of effort intensification is propelled by the disruptive force of enhanced wage expectations. During the transition to the higher level, before new standards have had time to become fixed, an inherently unstable situation is therefore inevitable. This alone would make it very difficult to ensure unchanging effort values. But we must also consider that the impetus towards change includes pressures from the external environment of the firm, and these in turn will tend to disrupt the prevailing expectations. If, to take an obvious example, the local supply of labour for a particular job (or industry) becomes scarce, the workers' expectations of tolerable effort will move towards looser rates because they are then in a position that offers more scope for restriction of output, working to rule, increasing absenteeism, unofficial strikes, and so forth. If, on the other hand, the supply of labour is abundant, expectations will gradually be adjusted in the opposite direction, towards tighter rates. Similar effects may come from the product market. When the market expands, and the firm's demand for labour grows, management may be compelled to attract labour by offering what amounts to relatively loose rates. And increasing competition in the product market means that the existing effort values have to be tightened up.

All this leads to the conclusion that the stability of effort values is bound to give way under the pressure of changing situations. Our next problem is therefore the question of movements in wage and effort levels that are *not* parallel, and to cope with its complexity we shall need a special concept. Taking a hypothetical equilibrium between effort and pay on a given level of expectations as an arbitrary starting point, to be called a situation of *wage parity*, non-parallel movements of the components of effort value may be described as various forms of wage *disparity*. Theoretically it is possible that effort intensity goes up and wages go down, or the opposite happens, and either process may occur at different levels of effort and wage expectations. But since all this is relative, it will suffice to confine the term 'wage disparity' to only one case, and here we should select the most realistic one. That is a situation in which both effort intensity and wages move towards a higher level but effort more so than wages. The result would be that effort value declines. Empirically, such a process corresponds exactly to the successful application of effort intensity controls (cp. Chapter 4). For it should be recalled that their function is to improve, from management's standpoint, labour effort per unit of wages.

A moment's reflection will show that we have now located the very centre of industrial conflict. As wages are costs to the firm, and the deprivations inherent in effort mean 'costs' to the employee, the interests of management and wage-earners are diametrically opposed in terms of the disparity process: a relative lowering of effort value is an advantage to management and a disadvantage to the workers, for it implies, by definition, that effort intensity per unit of wages is increased. We reach the conclusion, therefore, that not every changing situation is fraught with conflict, but only those which involve wage disparity. It should also be evident that any shift towards disparity, relative to an arbitrary point of origin, amounts to a re-distribution of the shares of the product between employer and worker in favour of the employer.

The statement that wage disparity is the central pivot of industrial conflict will need further comments to make it less abstract. To begin with, its truth is by no means impaired by the possibility that the participants in a particular conflict may not be aware of the change in effort values resulting from the disparity process. As a matter of fact, it is a striking characteristic of most wage disputes that they are conducted on the tacit assumption of effort intensity remaining constant. It is therefore interesting to look at different manifestations of unrest and strife in the light of varying degrees of awareness of wage disparity. Because many other factors are involved, only a broad, tentative view is possible and this would have to be modified according to varying conditions. Something like the following scale of potentially increasing awareness of wage disparity may be suggested, if only to illustrate the nature of the problem: major official strikes over national awards and industry-wide issues, unofficial strikes, excessive labour turnover, absenteeism, quota-restriction, goldbricking, and slowdowns.

In suggesting that strikes, especially official strikes on a large scale, are at one extreme, it must be borne in mind that within this category there may be variations according to type of industry, degree of unionization, and economic conditions. But by and large it seems true that wage rather than effort bargaining is the legitimate basis of strikes. The main purpose of the strike weapon, as it has been institutionalized inside the trade union movement, is to reinforce collective wage bargaining. And apart from such deviations as syndicalism, the main goals of trade unions have not contested the institution of employment as a system of effort controls. Thus, as far as strikes are concerned, work deprivations and therefore unchanging effort values are usually taken for granted so that the chief emphasis is on wages and general employment conditions. On analysis, however, since the concept of effort covers a wide range of deprivations, it is nevertheless true that every single strike ultimately must amount to a struggle over disparities in the relation of wages to effort. Several case studies have in fact reached similar conclusions, except that on the level of descriptive details clear-cut generalizations are rarely possible. But if one pierces through the welter of surface phenomena, at least certain phases of the disparity process are frequently observable.[1] According to what is perhaps the most typical pattern, the strike action begins as a response to a threatened or actual situation of increasing wage disparity and ends, if successful, by modifying, arresting, or reversing that process. The pattern can be significant even if a conflict expresses itself without any overt recognition of the role of effort standards or effort controls. For instance, the disputes

[1] See, in particular, W. Lloyd Warner and J. O. Low (1947); William Foote Whyte (1951); Liverpool University, Social Science Department (1954); A. Gouldner (1955).

that led to the strike in the shipbuilding and engineering industry of 1957 (see H. A. Clegg and Rex Adams, 1957) were ostensibly over the issue of 'wage-freezes' versus 'inflationary' wage
increases, with very little regard for the fact that inflation in-
evitably affects the national level of employment and thus the
overall effectiveness of the current system of effort controls.
Wage disparity is in any event more conscious and more articulated in the case of unofficial strike action. This type of conflict
is, as has been most carefully shown by Knowles (op. cit. 1951,
pp. 209ff.), in its underlying causes more directly associated with
an awareness that wages are a compensation for the deprivations and frustrations inherent in industrial effort.

This is still more apparent in excessive labour turnover as a
form of unrest. It has already been pointed out in Chapter 1 that
we have here a ceaseless search for the job in which wages
would fully compensate effort on the basis of prevailing standards. We can now add that the notoriously unstable occupations are a case of manifest wage disparity. The dominant
motives of these workers cannot be explained unless one as-
sumes that in fact they do compare potential earnings with required effort intensity. Absenteeism is on all counts very similar.
The decision to stay away from work at the expense of a loss in
earnings clearly implies that an unfavourable relation between
pay and effort is thereby, at least temporarily, re-adjusted.
Though this form of effort-withdrawal is as a rule not fully
conscious, it certainly requires some awareness of unsatisfactory
effort values. With quota-restriction, needless to say, wage disparity is clearly articulated in the worker's definition of the
situation; it becomes even more pronounced in the case of goldbricking and slowdowns. The disparity between effort and
earnings is then not only the dominant expectation, but is moreover combined with openly hostile attitudes towards the employer. The slowdown in particular is the strongest possible
expression of industrial strife because it is a highly deliberate
withdrawal of effort.

One advantage of including quite different symptoms of discon-
tent into the category of 'conflict' (as has also been suggested

by A. E. C. Hare (1958), pp. 77ff. and *passim*) is to remove the difficulty, which has often been encountered in empirical studies, that different symptoms (such as unofficial strikes and absenteeism) are to some extent interchangeable (Knowles (1952), pp. 225f.). The main point is, however, that this approach shows that the concept of wage disparity is applicable to all manifestations of conflict, even if the participants themselves are not aware of their conflicting interests in terms of changing effort values. In other words, we have thus obtained a criterion that is independent of whatever definition of the situation is in fact used by employees and employers in particular circumstances. The degree of awareness of disparities determines merely the overt manifestations of conflict, not its substance. The substance is always and necessarily a change in effort values that involves a modification of distributive shares. This has to be emphasized because the process of distribution is normally far too complex to be transparent to the participants in a given dispute. They can deal with the problem only by means of continuous trial and error until mutually satisfactory effort values have been obtained.

It follows that a valid analysis of industrial conflict on the basis of wage disparity must attempt to transcend the subjective definitions of the situation that are confined to particular issues; it must deal, instead, with the *system* of employer-employee relations as a whole. How, then, can we identify the objective factors that generally determine the extreme limits within which the process of wage disparity takes place? Here we meet an unexpected difficulty: the conditions of wage disparity seem to be over-determinate, for there are a number of forces that are more or less equally relevant in that sense. There is, for instance, the role of general economic policy around such issues as 'full employment' and 'redundancy'; variations in the overall level of employment, induced by national monetary policy, must, of course, have a tangible effect on the whole system of effort values. And there are other policies, although not centralized, which are similar in their aggregate effect on the relation between effort and wages. Typical examples are the utilization of

108

foreign labour, the propaganda for increased productivity, and the growing use of managerial controls over effort intensity. All these factors impinge upon wage disparity and at the same time transcend the individual firm. But they are too variable and diverse for the purpose of a general analysis. What we have to ascertain are the *extreme* limits that circumscribe for a given firm the scope of the disparity process. There are two major factors of this kind: the general economic situation and the socially prescribed pattern of work obligations. Both have the function of determining *marginal* disparity, that is to say, the extent to which disparity is accepted by the employee without causing any overt manifestations of conflict. To isolate these external boundaries of condoned disparity, we have to assume a margin of short-term flexibility of effort values in respect of individual firms. This is permissible because we are now concerned only with the main structural conditions of the system of effort values.

As regards economic conditions, the most relevant aspect is the effect of economic expansion conceived as a development towards increasingly large-scale production. In sociological inquiries, expanding firms are usually discussed against a background of technological, rather than economic, changes and thus the question of variations in distributive shares is not raised. This is understandable because to do so would make unavoidable trespass upon the grounds of economic analysis. There is, however, one relatively simple process that may be mentioned without touching on controversial issues of economic theory. Faced with an expanding product market, a firm may increase output (without necessarily enlarging the numbers employed or introducing technical innovations) simply by raising the average level of effort intensity. This would lead to an improved utilization of fixed capital assets. The expected economies make it possible to offer the employee, as an incentive to increased effort, a higher effort value and thus, *ceteris paribus*, a larger share in the product. This process is therefore relatively favourable to the employee; it amounts to a shift away from disparity towards parity. To generalize, we may conclude that the overall trend towards increased capital investment per unit of labour tends to diminish marginal wage disparity and thereby conditions the distributive process in favour of the employee.

By treating such economic factors as data, we can now turn to the social determinants of long-term variations in disparity. Let us dispose first of one possible but inadequate solution of the problem. It may seem obvious that an important set of factors impinging upon the system of effort values is the prevailing scope for upward social mobility. One might argue, for example, that if there was unrestricted mobility to the extent of full inter-changeability between employer and employee status, wage disparity could never persist for long. And conversely: the more powerful the barriers along the established status hierarchy, the larger is the margin for increasing wage disparity. It is true that these factors must have some effect in the long run on the dis-tribution of the product, via changes in the prevailing degree of disparity. But it can easily be seen that they constitute merely a necessary, not a sufficient, condition. For unlimited mobility could only lead to a general system of institutionalized parity if the conflicting interests of employers and employees (or of different status groups generally) were fully transparent so that comparisons of effort values in varying situations were possible. As we know, this is not the case. Although there is some aware-ness of effort values in certain manifestations of industrial con-flict, it appears to be limited to narrowly confined adjustments of effort and wages and rarely amounts to a recognition of the dis-tributive aspect of disparity processes.

Ultimately, therefore, the social foundations of marginally condoned disparity must be such factors as are themselves im-perceptible within the framework of conflicting interests; they must be invisible to the individuals or groups who confront each other, as employers and employees, with unavoidably conflict-ing aims. Now, as far as specifically social determinants of be-haviour are concerned, the only known factor that clearly fulfils that condition is the effect of social norms. As a product of socialization, norms are expectations that are unconsciously shared between otherwise differentiated groups. This takes us

110

back to the normative aspect of work obligations previously discussed (in Chapter 8). We identified the role of work obligations as a remote 'support' of industrial society which does not impinge directly upon the specific contents of the employment contract. But in the present context of marginal disparity conditions, the function of work obligations can be stated more precisely: though they cannot determine the concrete effort values in the course of changing situations, what they can do is to define the extreme *margin* of condoned disparity. Work obligations which in that sense surround the institution of employment are therefore just as much an external, objective force as the general economic conditions of large-scale production. The prevailing pattern of moral expectations that commands that industrial work is essentially an obligation is a determinant external to the individual. It prescribes his proper behaviour even if he is not aware of it; indeed, it is in that case all the more effective. And to accept work deprivations as a duty can only mean, in terms of the distributive process, that *to some extent* effort is surrendered to the employer free of compensation. The amount of free effort depends on the strength of the institutionally established norms of marginal disparity. In other words, the more powerful the employee's sense of obligation, the greater is the scope for increasing wage disparity in a given situation. The barriers to social mobility are, by comparison, of lesser importance. They constitute a protective stratum behind which a particular distribution of the product can maintain itself without interference from changes in the mechanism of occupational controls.

This conclusion implicitly provides an explanation for the shortcomings attached to the common-sense notion of 'efficiency'. The very fact that the criterion of efficient behaviour is the most widely accepted and most popular interpretation in all current approaches to problems of administration clearly points to normative expectations. Thus, in so far as the desirability of maximum efficiency is shared among employers and employees, it is an institutionalized goal having the same effect as work obligations. It is in fact merely a more generalized norm that

111

extends beyond the realm of industry into the universally accepted values of our society.

To go further we would need extensive empirical inquiries. Of particular interest would be the question whether there are developments which point beyond the contemporary framework of industrial conflict. Work obligations are at present still so firmly institutionalized that they are normally not experienced as a contradiction to the principle of effort compensation. Conscious withdrawal of effort, unlike the strike, is as yet not a legitimate weapon in industrial strife. Absenteeism, occupational instability, and restriction of output are so far merely the unintended and unexpressed by-products of the increased emphasis on the security of employment resulting from the use of monetary policies. It is however unquestionable that, with the continuous growth of large-scale organization, strikes tend to be less legitimate while, at the same time, effort withdrawal may well become more permissible. For the very methods that are the main administrative instrument of effort intensification, such as payment by results, make the process of effort compensation and, particularly, the relation of effort to earnings, more and more transparent. The growing preoccupation with the administration of effort values may thus possibly reach a point where the normative aspects of industrial work are less concealed or less taken for granted than at present. This would amount to a general drift in the institutional basis of employment from status to performance criteria. Unless a new pattern of social supports emerges, the disruptive effects of industrial conflict can then no longer be absorbed, as they have been hitherto, by the employee's tacit acceptance of work obligations.

The research hypotheses that suggest themselves along these lines are too numerous and too diverse to be mentioned in detail. Generally speaking, they should be most fruitful if concentrated on the institutional controls that determine or condition disparity processes in a concrete situation. Such an approach clearly implies that sociologists need no longer confine themselves to treating wages and salaries as status symbols only, thereby ignoring the role of effort values as an allegedly economic problem. In recognizing that these values, and the administrative controls connected with them, are a function of institutionalized expectations, which in turn are supported by social norms, they become automatically a legitimate subject for sociological inquiry.[1]

[1] An attempt to test the empirical usefulness of the concepts of wage-effort parity and disparity has been carried out by John C. McDonald (1958). It concerns problems of night shift work, investigated (chiefly) on the basis of a 10 per cent random sample of the production workers of a large manufacturing company. Starting off with the hypothesis that night shift presents normally a situation of wage parity because the additional hardships of such employment are balanced by extra earnings and other advantages, the inquiry led to unexpected results which were supported from insights gained by intensive case studies on a number of workers. It appeared that, apart from a few exceptionally privileged night-shift jobs, *dis*parity rather than parity was the characteristic situation for the majority of the night-shift workers. Significantly, this was effectively concealed by various rationalizations and projections which the workers maintained to reconcile themselves with the coercive nature of the prevailing conditions.

CHAPTER 11

The Size of Effort Value

THE CONCLUSION reached in the last chapter would appear to dissent from the opinions prevalent today among industrial sociologists. We have placed the main emphasis of the analysis on the existence of a fundamental disparity between the worker's effort and his wages, a disparity that is negative from his point of view: his sacrifices are greater than his gains. This means that industrial organization is inherently unjust, for the conditions that create wage disparity—limited upward mobility and institutionalized work obligations—are part of the larger social system. Before we go on with the analysis, a few words in defence of an apparently unpopular conclusion may therefore not be out of place.

Wage disparity implies that industrial unrest is the most important, most characteristic feature of industrial organization. This in turn is due to the supposition that the interests of employers and employees are diametrically opposed because they concern the distribution of the product. Not many years ago, such a point of view would have been quite unacceptable. The main contention among sociologists then was that, since conflict was the result of misunderstandings and lack of 'communication' between management and workers, it was avoidable. But intensified empirical studies have made this position untenable. It became increasingly clear that, in spite of the improvements in human relations that might have been possible, a substantial residual of industrial conflict is inevitable. It is now fairly generally accepted that there are, in addition to common interests, 'areas of competition', 'differences in goals', and 'conflicting objectives' between wage-earners and management.[1] So that it is

[1] For a representative summary of this trend see C. M. Arensberg *et al.* (1957), e.g. Wilensky, p. 40–43; L. Sayles, p. 42–45; cp. also H. Blumer (1954).

only in degree that our analysis departs from accepted views.

Even so, there are very obvious facts that still bar the way towards a full recognition of the dichotomous nature of industrial organization. However plausible on theoretical-analytical grounds the divergence of interests may be, it remains puzzling why so much of it seems to disappear as soon as one approaches the concrete setting of routine industrial relations. What is it that obscures the logic of irreconcilable conflict underlying the disparity process? It is, no doubt, partly due to the camouflage resulting from the managerial manipulation of workers' attitudes and beliefs. For one of the functions of the morale-builder's techniques is to conceal from the worker precisely those managerial objectives which amount to increased wage disparity. We may recall here, in particular, that salesmanship is considered as an important skill for the time-study man. But there is no way of assessing the long-term effectiveness of these controls. We can merely presume that they must have some effect because they are—despite their costliness—increasingly used.

But there is another factor that is more obviously effective in concealing the role of disparity. Variations in effort value affect not only the relation between employer and employee, but also the relations among the employees themselves. If the difference between good and bad jobs in a given plant increases, a good deal of friction between workers arises. In due course these pressures lead to a more evenly balanced structure of effort values. Obviously this has nothing to do with the average size of effort values in that plant. So these two aspects must be kept strictly apart (cf. schema on p. 11). It is characteristic of the structural aspect that there is not necessarily a conflict over it between management and workers; both sides are usually interested in an even distribution of effort values from job to job. It is the size rather than the structure of effort value that reflects the clash of interests. We must realize that each situation may at any time be interpreted in terms of *either* the structure *or* the size of effort values. It depends on the prevailing circumstances. In an atmosphere of industrial peace, the participants will be preoccupied with minor tensions between different sections of employees. During a strike, on the other hand, these frictions over the structure of effort in relation to earnings will be displaced by a concern over the size of effort value. The focus of conflict thus centres on a struggle between employer and employee over the control of wage disparity. The existence of conflicting definitions of the situation presents no special problems for a sociological analysis. It is simply a case of the familiar paradigm of latent and manifest functions. The importance of the dual aspect of effort value—structure and size—is this. Under conditions that favour a preponderance of internal conflicts between different employers, occupations, and unions these issues may tend to overshadow the more fundamental dichotomy between employer and employee. It is well known that such conditions are typical of the more highly advanced industrial societies. The whole development of modern trade unionism is characterized by its increasing preoccupation with disruptive sectional interests. From the social analyst's standpoint it is, of course, perfectly legitimate to study a given situation in terms of the size aspect of effort value even when this aspect remains latent because the predominant emphasis of the people involved is on the structural aspect.

Up to now we have only been concerned with the scope of wage disparity. To continue the analysis, we shall take as given a certain scope of disparity, determined by the combined effect of work obligations and limited upward mobility. The problem then is to explain variations in disparity *within this scope*. In view of the complexity of the matter the use of a geometrical presentation will be advisable. The diagram (p. 117) shows the relation of effort to wages by assuming that both variable reflect homogeneous quantities.[1] On the central dotted line, running at an angle of 45°, every point represents a job in which the amount of effort equals the amount of wages: along this line, we therefore have a situation of wage-parity. Above it, wages are everywhere greater than effort; here the disparity between effort and

[1] To visualize effort as a homogeneous quantity, it should be noted that in practice *relative* variations in effort are all that is needed to create a problem; these may be recognized as variations in hours of work, pace of work in terms of output per man hour, etc.

116

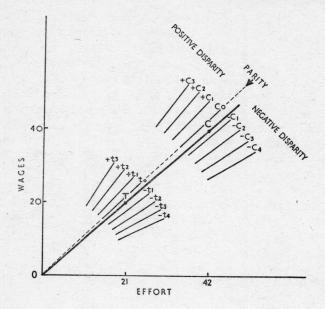

wages is 'positive', that is, favourable from the employee's point of view. Below the central line, the disparity is 'negative'. Thus, the line OC presents a particular degree of negative wage disparity, the size of which is measured by the angle which this line forms with the central line. It is evident that all straight lines that run through zero depict a constant relation between effort and wages or, in other words, a balanced structure of effort value. Now, in order to concentrate on the size aspect alone, we must ignore the structural aspect and we may do that by assuming that there is sufficient labour mobility between different jobs to ensure equal effort value among all jobs. All disparity lines will then run through zero. Next we must eliminate what we previously called the 'level' of effort values. This appears as the distance between a given point on any one line and zero: the greater the distance, the higher the level of effort value. For example, at C wages and effort are on the level of 40/42, while at

117

T the level is 20/21. This difference in level of effort value may be illustrated by visualizing C and T as average effort values in two contrasting industries, such as Coal and Textiles. But the concept 'level of effort value' is also useful in describing the finer differentiation of wage and effort levels within a given firm. The short lines t_0, t_1, t_2, etc., and c_0, c_1, c_2, etc., represent such differentiations: the longer these lines are, the larger is the variation of effort value levels within the firm. It should be noticed though, that differences in occupational costs, according to length of training, are not shown in this diagram, which means that we are assuming here that all firms employ workers with the same level of skill (cp. p. 33 above). Finally, we can introduce the dimension of time by interpreting the succession of short lines at a given average level (at T or C) as a sequence of points in time. A process of increasing either positive or negative disparity, for example, is shown by the succession of t_0, t_1, t_2, and so on.

With these assumptions, which help to simplify the matter, we are able to obtain an accurate description of variations in the size of effort value over a wide range of possible cases. By combining changes in the relative movement of wages and effort, we may distinguish twelve paradigmatic cases, as follows:

1. Wages increase, effort decreases (irrelevant in practice).
2. Wages increase, effort remains constant (e.g., as result of rising productivity through technical innovations).
3. Wages remain constant, effort decreases (e.g., through reduction in hours of work).
4. Wages increase, effort increases less than proportionally (e.g., 'progressive' system of piece rates: frequently also during changeover from day rates to piecework).
5. Wages decrease, effort decreases more than proportionally (practically not very relevant).
6. Wages increase, effort increases over-proportionally (e.g., 'degressive' system of piecework; possible also through 'measured daywork' by means of day rates above the going rate).

7. Wages decrease, effort decreases less than proportionally (possible by means of concealed rate-cutting).
8. Wages constant, effort increases (possible through manipulation of employee attitudes).
9. Wages decrease, effort constant (e.g., during depression).
10. Wages decrease, effort increases (irrelevant in practice).
11. Wages and effort increase proportionally (through introduction of piecework, etc.).
12. Wages and effort decrease proportionally (possible during depression, particularly if combined with reduced hours of work).

The first five cases illustrate positive disparities, the second five are cases of negative disparity, while the last two are situations of wage parity. Although we are dealing here with hypothetical constructions, it will be seen from the illustrations added in brackets that there are several cases that approximate to relevant practical situations.

The factors that generally determine changes in the size of effort value are easily ascertained on this basis. All those forces which strengthen the bargaining position of the employer will tend to shift the lines in the diagram downwards, i.e. from positive towards negative disparity, while the opposite holds for any improvement in the bargaining position of the employee. Thus, during an economic depression, there will be a movement downwards; but an increase in trade-union power will result in a shift upwards from, say, $-t_3$ to $-t_2$ and so on. Combined changes in level and size of effort value will appear as follows: if piece-rates or excessive day-rates are introduced by means of a trial period, the process will normally mean that effort values are first increased, then move towards a higher level, and finally, on that level, back again to a position of decreased effort value. For instance, $-t_1$ shifts to $+ t_1$, from there upwards towards $+ c_1$ and then to $-c_1$. This would be the case of the stringency pattern based on a favourable bargaining position of the employer. If, however, the situation is favourable to the employee, the process would stop somewhere between $+ t_1$ and $+ c_1$.

I

The relative strength of the bargaining position therefore appears as a specific determinant of effort value. It should be noted here that this mechanism is restricted by the remote boundaries that prescribe the scope of wage disparity: the economic and social environment of the plant. In the long run even the most pronounced changes in bargaining strength cannot of course transcend these boundaries. An interesting example of this is the situation of full (or 'overfull') employment, induced by inflationary policies. The most obvious effect is an overall improvement in the wage-earner's bargaining position, with the familiar results of absenteeism, declining factory discipline, increased wage demands, and so on, all of which amount to a general shift towards positive disparity. In the long run, however, this movement must stop short at the boundary set by the economic needs of the firm's survival. 'Positive' disparity is only possible for short periods of time at the expense of the firm's capital reserves. Profit margins become so small that the employer has to withdraw his capital in order to consume it or invest it elsewhere. In the case of nationalized industries the managerial salaries and privileges will be so reduced that management will be induced to leave the industry. The overall effect will be a general decline in productivity and hence a shrinkage of the national income. The opposite will tend to occur, *mutatis mutandis*, in a situation of less than full employment.

These problems unavoidably touch upon certain aspects of economic analysis, which clearly transcend the sociologist's competence. We can do no more than point out the approximate place where any further step in the analysis would require the co-operation of an economist. The gains from such co-operation need not be altogether one-sided. It is feasible that economic analysis, too, may derive some advantage from it. For example, the variations in effort value may possibly have some relevance to the problem of economic growth. Wage-disparity may be interpreted as a form of profit that originates in a particular type of industrial organization, as a result of institutional controls. Whether, and to what extent, these profits are whittled away by competition in the product market (to the consumer's

120

advantage) need not concern us. The point is that *some* measure of negative wage-disparity appears in our analysis as a permanent institutional condition of industrial enterprise, and this may facilitate the analysis of the growth processes. That is to say, the whole system appears to have an inherent propensity towards expansion. Institutional forces which, on the other hand, lead to a decline in or to the disappearance of negative wage-disparity indicate a situation of stability or even general decline of the economic system. For all practical purposes it would therefore be justifiable to consider negative disparity as the normal situation in an expanding economy. Other factors in economic development, such as technological and organizational innovation, can thus be treated as dependent variables, which are a function of wage-disparity. Thus, if a given degree of wage-disparity declines as a result of institutional changes, this would be a stimulus to innovation. We may bring to mind here the familiar argument, traditionally advanced by American trade unionists, that high wages lead to technical progress; with the important proviso, however, that what really matters is not high wages but high effort values. Generally speaking, a recognition of the fundamental role of changing effort values might facilitate a more comprehensive approach to the problems of economic growth, stability, and decline.

However, this does not mean that we are now handing the analysis over to economics at the point where it becomes unmanageably complex. Certainly a systematic treatment of the interlocking of social and economic processes would require a far more sophisticated approach than is possible within the compass of the few selected variables we have used. What it does mean is that we have to stop short of problems that are no longer strictly relevant to our subject-matter, the field of industrial organization. We have, in fact, reached that limitation to sociological inquiry which is commonly referred to as the 'economic environment' of the social system of employer-employee relations (cp. A. Siegel, 1957). But we have succeeded in going further than has hitherto been possible. We have not merely argued that the 'internal' system of in-plant social relations is—

121

somewhere—surrounded by economic conditions whose precise effect is unknown. We have shown that the internal system revolves centrally on effort values. This produced a direct link between the micro- and macro-sociological dimensions. For the controls of effort and wages in the plant are inseparably interlocked with the wider processes of effort and wage evaluation, processes that originate in the external social and economic milieux of the plant. In other words, these factors do not have a remote conditioning effect on the autonomous system of social relations in the workshop, but operate as specific determinants of these relations.[1]

[1] For a further development of this approach see W. Baldamus (1960).

SUMMARY

THE PURPOSE of this study has been to supplement the current approach to industrial organization by an analysis of industrial administration, centred on the concepts of efficiency and effort. We found that inquiries into this field are at present severely limited by a theoretical postulate that is inadequate: the assumption that the prevailing system of industrial relations reveals a natural harmony of interests between employers and employees. Conflicts and tensions are, on that basis, merely the by-product of minor rigidities and superficial imperfections in the working of the market mechanism. If, instead, these relations are conceived in terms of fundamentally opposed interests, the problem of efficient industrial administration immediately becomes more significant. For the main issue then becomes a problem that, despite its importance, has as yet never been solved: the distribution of earned income between management and wage-earners. There appear to be two factors that determine this distribution, the structure of occupational costs (connected with the mechanism of the labour market) and the administrative process by which management controls the efficiency of labour. We discovered that, although administrative controls play a far more important role than do occupational costs, they have been persistently neglected in past research. As industrial administration is a complex network of managerial controls over the wage-earner's effort, and as 'effort' is—apparently—a highly unstable phenomenon, a sufficiently rigorous analysis has so far not been possible. To make it possible would necessitate the reduction of all these things to a system of relatively simple yet comprehensive properties.

We proceeded by dividing the whole area of administrative effort controls, ranging from employee supervision to methods of wage payment and methods of production, into two broad

123

categories, *stability* and *intensity* controls. The first stabilizes the relation of effort to earnings in a given situation. The function of the other is to raise the level of effort per unit of wages. As the distinction between stability and intensity of effort is an analytical one, it makes no difference that in practice the two types of control are frequently intermixed. (In payment by results, for example, the change-over from daywork to piecework is usually at first a means of effort intensity control; but once piecework has been accepted, its main purpose is then to secure stability of effort levels.) Further inquiry pointed to an unsolved problem connected with the administration of effort intensity. While the control of stability is possible on the basis of prevailing habitual standards of effort, the manipulation of effort intensity requires precise and clearly articulated expectations of what is the 'right' level of effort. But such expectations seemed to be derived from nothing more objective than the intuitive judgement and the practical experience of the administrator.

Clearly, then, some advance, however tentative, towards an analysis of effort components is badly needed. Three main elements, defined as different aspects of the deprivation inherent in industrial work, appeared fairly obvious: *impairment, tedium,* and *weariness* (or 'fatigue'). In putting the emphasis on deprivation, we would seem to contradict an interpretation of industrial work that has had considerable appeal to managerial executives and professional people: the notion that wage-earners, even at the lower levels of skill, find a great deal of 'satisfaction' in their occupation. However, when one looks more closely into the matter, such satisfactions reveal themselves as more or less illusory. They are largely substitute goals or rationalizations which are a function of deprivation, not an independent variable in the motivation to work. As a result, the components of effort remain psychologically exceedingly complex and unstable. The only objective aspect turns on the fact that the deprivational elements are a response to specific work realities such as distasteful physical conditions, stultifying repetitiveness, and coercive routines.

To take the analysis further, social factors which underpin the motivation to work have to be incorporated. In the first place, particular motives may become relatively stable if they are supported by moral attitudes that are acquired in early childhood and become part of an individual's personality structure. On that basis they develop into habitually maintained standards and norms of conduct. An important product of this institutionalization is the deeply rooted sense of obligation which, in industrial society, permeates the whole sphere of occupational activities. But although *obligations to work* are a powerful factor providing a measure of stability to industrial organization, their effects on effort expectations are remote and diffuse. Certain observations indicate that their strength varies in a number of ways, notably according to class origin and social status.

Closely connected with work obligations, but comparatively more articulated, is another stabilizing factor: the *standardization of effort* in the course of prolonged and unvaried activities. It explains the existence of surprisingly rigid standards of 're-quired' effort in the context of industrial administration. The substance of these standards are expectations among wage-earners and managers of what is right or wrong, too much or too little, in terms of effort intensity. Several investigations have shown that this kind of institutionalized expectation prescribes the wage-earner's conduct within fairly close bounds. Moreover, such standards obtain still more stability and even some degree of precision as they tend to be projected into similarly standardized wage expectations. Thus, wage and effort expectations are, through this remarkable process, interlocked. Specific jobs, operations, and wage rates are normatively defined as 'good' or 'bad', 'loose' or 'tight' according to whether a relatively fixed goal of earnings may be secured by little or much effort. This standardization of *effort values*, then, is the institutional basis that so effectively facilitates predictability and control of the wage-earner's effort. It reveals a strange world of intricately mixed, highly organized, and yet morally compulsive expectations, a world of which nothing was known to the outsider until a few years ago. Most of the factual evidence on characteristic procedures and practices has come from observations on

125

the administration of piecework, particularly on restriction of output, rate-cutting, and methods of time-study. But it can easily be shown that, independently of the methods of wage payment, the interlocking of standardized effort and wage expectations in the form of effort values governs the entire realm of administrative controls within the institution of employment.

But for all their rigidity under stationary conditions, effort values are bound to give way under the prolonged pressure of economic and social changes in the external environment of the firm. The problem of long-term flexibility becomes clearer if account is taken of variations in the *level* of effort values. Accordingly, movements in wage and effort expectations may or may not be parallel, and the relevant situations thus reflect either wage-effort *parity* or wage-effort *disparity*. The case of wage disparity is of special interest to an analysis of efficient industrial administration. For, taken as a whole, a necessary condition for successful administration is to increase the level of average effort so that this advantage to the employer is not entirely offset by a corresponding rise in wages or by provoking disturbances resulting in industrial conflict. Logically, therefore, the dominant goal of management is to achieve, increase, or maintain *marginal* wage disparity, short of manifest conflicts. The worker's dominant striving, on the other hand, is to preserve wage parity. This conclusion, however, demands a wider interpretation of industrial strife than is customary. Not only strikes, but other kinds of instability including absenteeism, excessive labour turnover, and restriction of output have to be defined as symptoms of a fundamental discrepancy in the relation of effort to wages.

Ultimately there are two groups of factors that prescribe the extreme limits within which condoned disparity may persist as a result of effective effort controls. The first group appears as the economic environment of the firm, and here we found the process of intensive capital utilization most important for an analysis of the relative shares of management and wage-earners of specific productivity gains. The second set of limiting factors takes the analysis back to the role of work obligations. The more strongly these are institutionalized, the greater is the scope for
126

retaining wage disparity within the margin of peaceful industrial relations.

But the analysis of the scope of marginal disparity can deal only with major factors in long-term development. In the short run, it is the *size* of effort value within a given scope of disparity that has to be explored. A comparatively rigorous treatment of this problem becomes possible by introducing a further simplification. If we assume perfect mobility between wage-earners from job to job, there will be a balanced *structure* of equitable effort values such that all jobs are equally bad (or equally good) from the standpoint of the employee. The size of effort value emerges then as the sole object of conflicting interests between employer and employee in the short run: the former strives to lower and the latter to raise the value. By combining variations in the size of effort value with changes in the level of effort value, a fairly realistic description of a wide range of industrial situations emerges. The pattern of these situations is determined by the relative bargaining strength of employers and employees. The analysis links up at this point with observations and concepts that are already familiar through the conventional treatment of industrial conflict. Thus we can see here that a great deal of what is common knowledge in this field can be systematized by identifying short-term variations in the size of effort value as the crucial variable. At the same time, we can appreciate the way in which these problems have been oversimplified in previous research and theoretical work—neither the size, level, nor structure of effort values was taken into consideration.

As to future empirical research, the most promising approach would be to obtain further insight into the nature of industrial conflict as it is affected by long-term changes in the institutional framework of industrial administration. The present study has shown that the apparent complexity of such problems can be effectively reduced by demonstrating that the one strategic factor in industrial efficiency is the institutionalized relation of effort to wages.

REFERENCES

ACTON SOCIETY TRUST. *Size and Morale*. London, 1953.

ALLEN, V. L. 'Incentives in the Building Industry.' *Economic Journal*, **63**, 1952.

ARENSBERG, CONRAD M. *et al*. (ed.) *Research in Industrial Human Relations*. New York, 1957.

BALCHIN, NIGEL. 'Satisfactions in Work'. *Occup. Psychol.*, **21**, 1947.

BALDAMUS, W. *Incentives and Work Analysis*. Monograph A I, University of Birmingham, 1951a.

BALDAMUS, W. 'Type of Work and Motivation.' *Brit. J. Sociol.*, 1951b.

BALDAMUS, W. 'Mechanization, Utilization and Size of Plant.' *Econ. J.*, **63**, 1953.

BALDAMUS, W. 'A Sociological Theory of Economic Administration.' *Brit. J. Sociol.*, **8**, 1957a.

BALDAMUS, W. 'The Relationship between Wage and Effort.' *J. indus. Econ.*, **6**, 1957b.

BALDAMUS, W. *Der gerechte Lohn*. Berlin, 1960.

BALDAMUS, W. and BEHREND, H. 'Variations in Absenteeism during the Week: an Index of Employee Morale.' *Nature*, **165**, 1950.

BALDAMUS, W. and TIMMS, NOEL. 'The Problem Family: A Sociological Approach.' *Brit. J. Sociol.*, **6**, 1955.

BARMACK, J. E. 'The Effect of Benzedrine Sulphate (benzyl methyl carbinamine) upon the Report of Boredom and other Factors.' *J. Psychol.*, **5**, 1938.

BARNARD, CHESTER I. *The Functions of the Executive*. Cambridge, Mass., 1938.

BARTLEY, HOWARD and CHUTE, ELOISE. *Fatigue and Impairment in Man*. New York and London, 1947.

129

References

BEHREND, HILDE. *Absence under Full Employment.* Monograph A 3, University of Birmingham, 1951.

BEHREND, HILDE. 'Absence and Labour Turnover in a Changing Economic Climate.' *Occup. Psychol.*, **27**, 1953.

BEHREND, HILDE. 'The Effort Bargain.' *Indus. and Labor Relat. Rev.*, **10**, 1957.

BEWS, B. I. M. 'An Experimental Investigation of the Concept of Psychical Satiation.' M.A. Thesis, Cornell University, 1951.

BLUMER, HERBERT. 'Social Structure and Power Conflict.' In: *Industrial Conflict*, ed. by A. Kornhauser, R. Dubin, and Arthur M. Ross. New York, 1954.

BRITISH INSTITUTE OF MANAGEMENT. *Wage Incentive Schemes.* London, 1950.

BÜCHER, KARL. *Arbeit und Rhytmus.* 5th ed. Leipzig, 1919.

CENTERS, RICHARD. 'Motivational Aspects of Occupational Stratification.' *J. Soc. Psychol.*, **28**, 1948.

CHINOY, ELY. *Automobile Workers and the American Dream.* New York, 1955.

CLEGG, H. A. and FLANDERS, ALLAN, *The System of Industrial Relations in Great Britain.* Oxford, 1954.

CLEGG, H. A. and ADAMS, REX. *The Employer's Challenge.* Oxford, 1957.

COASE, R. H. 'The Nature of the Firm.' *Economica*, **4**, 1937.

COLE, G. D. H. *The Case for Industrial Partnership.* London, 1957.

COX, DAVID and DYCE, K. M. 'Research on the Unit of Work.' *Occup. Psychol.*, **25**, 1951.

COX, DAVID, DYCE-SHARP K. M. and IRVINE, D. H. *Women's Attitudes to Repetitive Work.* Nat. Inst. Industrial Psychology. London, 1953.

CRAWFORD, J. 'The Problem of Introducing Modern Systems of Wage Payment into the Boot and Shoe Industry.' *J. Indus. Econ.*, **1**, 1953.

DALTON, MELVILLE. 'The Industrial Ratebuster.' *Appl. Anthropol.*, **7**, 1948.

130

DAVIS, NORAH M. 'Attitudes to Work: A Field Study of Building Operatives.' *Brit. J. Psychol.*, **38**, 1948.

DAVIS, NORAH M. 'Some Psychological Conflicts Caused by Group Bonus Methods of Payment.' *Brit. J. Indus. Med.*, **10**, 1953.

DERBER, MILTON. *Labor-Management Relations at the Plant Level under Industry-wide Bargaining*. University of Illinois, 1955.

DOUGLAS, PAUL. *The Theory of Wages*. New York, 1934.

DURKHEIM, EMILE. *The Division of Labour in Society*. (Trans. S. G. Simpson). Glencoe, 1947.

ELIAS, NORBERT. 'Problems of Involvement and Detachment.' *Brit. J. Sociol.*, **8**, 1956.

VON FERBER, CHRISTIAN. *Arbeitsfreude, Wirklichkeit und Ideologie*. Stuttgart, 1959.

VON FERBER, CHRISTIAN. 'Interessenpluralismus und Empirische Sozialforschung.' *Zeitschr. für Politik*, **51**, 1958.

FLUGEL, J. C. *Man, Morals and Society*. London, 1945.

FLUGEL, J. C. 'L'appétit vient en mangeant. Some Reflections on the Self-sustaining Tendencies.' *Brit. J. Psychol.*, **38**, 1947.

FREUD, ANNA. *The Ego and the Mechanisms of Defence*. London, 1937.

FRIEDMANN, GEORGES. *Ou va le Travail Humain?* Librairie Gallimard, 1950.

FÜRSTENBERG, FRIEDRICH. 'Die Soziale Funktion der Leistungsanreize (Incentives) im Industriebetrieb.' *Kölner Zeitschrift für Soziologie*, **7**, 1955.

FÜRSTENBERG, FRIEDRICH. *Probleme der Lohnstruktur*. Tübingen, 1958.

GOLDHAMER, H. and SHILS, EDWARD A., 'Types of Power and Status.' *Amer. J. Sociol.*, **45**, 1939.

GOULDNER, ALVIN W. *Wildcat Strike. A Study of an Unofficial Strike*. London, 1955.

GRACIE, J. J. *A Fair Day's Pay*. London, 1949.

HALL, PATRICIA and LOCKE, N. W. *Incentives and Contentment*. London, 1938.

References

HARE, A. E. C. *The First Principles of Industrial Relations.* London, 1958.

HICKS, J. R. *The Theory of Wages.* London, 1932.

HYMAN, HERBERT H. 'The Value Systems of Different Classes: A Social Psychological Contribution to the Analysis of Stratification.' In: *Class, Status and Power,* ed. by R. Bendix and S. M. Lipset. Glencoe, Ill., 1953.

INTERNATIONAL LABOUR OFFICE. *Payment by Results.* Geneva, 1951.

JAHODA, M. 'Some Socio-Psychological Problems of Factory Life and Contentment.' *Brit. J. Psychol.,* **32,** 1941.

JAQUES, ELLIOTT. *The Changing Culture of a Factory.* London, 1951.

KENNEDY, VAN DUSEN. *Union Policy and Incentive Wage Methods.* New York, 1945.

KEYNES, JOHN MAYNARD. *The General Theory of Employment, Interest and Money.* London, 1936.

KNOWLES, K. G. J. C. 'Some Notes on Engineering Earnings.' *Bulletin of the Oxford University Institute of Statistics,* **13, 7,** 1951.

KNOWLES, K. G. J. C. *Strikes: A Study in Industrial Conflict.* Oxford, 1952.

KRAEPELIN, E. 'Die Arbeitskurve.' *Philosophische Studien,* **19,** Leipzig, 1902.

LEWIN, KURT. 'A Dynamic Theory of Personality.' *Selected Papers.* New York and London, 1935.

LEWIN, KURT and KARSTEN, A. 'Untersuchungen zur Handlungs- und Affektpsychologie: V. Psychische Sättigung.' *Psychologische Forschungen,* **10,** 1928.

LIVERPOOL UNIVERSITY, SOCIAL SCIENCE DEPARTMENT. *The Dockworker. An Analysis of Conditions of Employment in the Port of Manchester.* Liverpool, 1954.

LONG, JOYCE. *Labour Turnover under Full Employment.* Monograph A II., University of Birmingham, 1951.

LOWE, ADOLPH. *Economics and Sociology.* London, 1935.

References

LOWE, ADOLPH. 'On the Mechanistic Approach in Economics.' *Soc. Res.* **18,** 1951.

LOWRY, S. M., MAYNARD, H. B. and STEGEMERTEN, G. J. *Time and Motion Study.* 3rd. ed. New York, 1940.

LUPTON, TOM and CUNNISON, SHEILA. 'The Cash Reward for an Hour's Work under three Piecework Incentive Schemes.' *The Manchester School,* **25,** 1957.

LYMAN, ELIZABETH L. 'Occupational Differences in the Value Attached to Work.' *Amer. J. Sociol.,* **61,** 1955.

MACE, C. A. 'Incentives: Some Experimental Studies.' I.H.R.B., **72,** 1935.

MACE, C. A. 'Human Relations in the Building Industry.' *Occup. Psychol.,* **24,** 1950.

MACE, C. A. *Introspection and Analysis,* ed. by Max Black. Ithaca, New York, 1950b.

MCDONALD, JOHN C. 'Social and Psychological Aspects of Night Shift Work.' Ph. D. Thesis, University of Birmingham, 1958.

MAIER, NORMAN R. F. *Principles of Human Relations.* New York, 1952.

MARSHALL, THOMAS. *Citizenship and Social Class.* Cambridge, 1950.

MERTON, ROBERT K. and KITT, ALICE S. 'Contributions to the Theory of Reference Group Behavior.' In: *Continuities in Social Research,* ed. by R. K. Merton and Paul Lazarsfield. Glencoe, Ill., 1950.

MILLER, DELBERT C. and FORM, WILLIAM H. *Industrial Sociology.* New York, 1951.

MILLS, C. WRIGHT. *The Contribution of Sociology to Studies of Industrial Relations.* Industrial Relations Research Association. Champaign, Ill., 1949.

MILLS, C. WRIGHT. *White Collar: The American Middle Classes.* New York, 1951.

MINISTRY OF WORKS. *Payment by Results in Building and Civil Engineering during the War.* H.M.S.O., 1947.

MOORE, WILBERT E. *Industrial Relations and the Social Order.* 2nd. ed. New York, 1951.

133

References

PARSONS, TALCOTT. *The Social System.* Glencoe, Ill., 1951.

PARSONS, TALCOTT, BALES, R. F., and SHILS, E. A. *Working Papers in the Theory of Action.* Glencoe, Ill., 1953.

PARSONS, TALCOTT, BALES, R. F., *et al. Family, Socialization and Interaction Process.* Glencoe, Ill., 1955.

PARSONS, TALCOTT and SMELSER, NEIL J. *Economy and Society.* London, 1956.

PIPPING, H. *Standard of Living. The Concept and its Place in Economics.* Copenhagen, 1953.

PRESGRAVE, RALPH. *The Dynamics of Time Study.* 2nd ed. New York, 1945.

REYNOLDS, LLOYD G. *Labor Economics and Labor Relations.* New York, 1949.

RICE, A. K., HILL, J. M. M., and TRIST, E. L. 'The Representation of Labour Turnover as a Social Process.' *Hum. Relat.,* 3, 1950, 4, 1951, 5, 1952, 6, 1953.

RIESMAN, DAVID *et al. The Lonely Crowd .* New Haven, 1950.

ROBBINS, LIONEL *An Essay on the Nature and Signficance of Economic Science.* London, 1937.

ROBERTSON, D. H. *Control of Industry.* London, 1923.

RODGERS, WINSTON and HAMMERSLEY, J. M. 'The Consistency of Stop-Watch Time-Study Practitioners.' *Occup. Psychol.,* 28, 1954.

ROETHLISBERGER, F. J. and DICKSON, WILLIAM J. *Management and the Worker.* Cambridge, Mass., 1939.

ROY, DONALD. 'Quota Restriction and Goldbricking in a Machine Shop.' *Amer. J. Sociol.,* 57, 1952.

RYAN, THOMAS ARTHUR. *Work and Effort. The Psychology of Production.* New York, 1947.

RYAN, THOMAS ARTHUR and CAIN SMITH, PATRICIA. *Principles of Industrial Psychology.* New York, 1954.

SALKEYER, LOUIS R. 'Towards a Theory of Wage Structure.' *Int. Lab. Relat. Rev.,* 6, 1953.

SAYLES, LEONARD R. 'Work Group Behavior and the Larger Organization,' in: Arensberg, *et al.,* 1957.

SCHNEIDER, EUGENE V. *Industrial Sociology*. New York, 1957.

SHERIF, MUSAFER. *The Psychology of Social Norms*. New York and London, 1936.

SHULTZ, GEORGE P. *Pressures on Wage Decisions*. Cambridge, Mass., 1951.

SIEGEL, ABRAHAM J. 'The Economic Environment in Human Relations Research', in: C. M. Arensberg, *et al.*, 1957.

SIMMEL, GEORG. *The Sociology of Georg Simmel*. Translated and edited by Kurt H. Wolff. Glencoe, Ill., 1950.

SIMON, HERBERT A. *Administrative Behavior*. New York, 1946.

SMITH, P. C. and LEM. C. 'Effects of Lot Size upon Spacing of Voluntary Rest Periods.' *Amer. Psychologist*, **8**, 1953.

STIGLER, GEORGE J. *The Theory of Price*. New York, 1947.

STOUFFER, S. A., SUCHMAN, E. A., *et al. The American Soldier*. Vol. **1**, of *Studies in Social Psychology in World War II*, ed. by F. Osborn, *et al.* Princeton, 1949.

TEAD, ORDWAY and METCALF, H. C. *Personnel Administration*. London, 1933.

TIMMS, NOEL. 'Social Standards and the Problem Family.' *Case Conference*, **2**, 1956.

TURNER, H. A. 'Trade Unions, Differentials and the Levelling of Wages.' *The Manchester School*, **20**, 1952.

VERNON, H. M. *Industrial Fatigue and Efficiency*. London, 1921.

VERNON, H. M., WYATT, S. and OGDEN, A. D. 'On the Extent and Effects of Variety in Repetitive Work.' I.F.R.B., **26**, 1924.

WALKER, C. R. 'The Problem of the Repetitive Job.' *Harvard Business Rev.*, **28**, 1950.

WALKER, C. R. 'Work Methods, Working Conditions and Morale.' In: *Industrial Conflict*, ed. by A. Kornhauser, R. Dubin, and A. M. Ross, New York, 1954.

WALKER, C. R. and GUEST, ROBERT H. *The Man on the Assembly Line*. Cambridge, Mass., 1952.

WARNER, W. LLOYD and LOW, J. O. *The Social System of the Modern Factory*. Yale University Press, 1947.

K

References

WEBER, MAX. 'Zur Psychophysik der industriellen Arbeit.' *Archiv für Sozialwissenschaft und Sozialpolitik*, **27**, 1908, **28**, and **29**, 1909.

WESTON, H. C. and ADAMS, S. 'The Effects of Noise on the Performance of Weavers.' I.H.R.B. No. 65, 1932.

WILENSKY, HAROLD L. 'Human Relations in the Workplace: An Appraisal of Some Recent Research,' in: C. M. Arensberg, *et al.*, 1957.

WOOTTON, BARBARA. *The Social Foundations of Wage Policy.* London, 1955.

WYATT, S. and FRASER, J. A. 'Studies in Repetitive Work with Special Reference to Rest Pauses.' I.F.R.B. No. 32. 1925.

WYATT, S., FRASER, Y. A. and STOCK, F. G. L. 'The Effects of Monotony in Work.' I.F.R.B. No. 56, 1929.

WYATT, S. and LANGDON, J. N. 'The Machine and the Worker.' I.H.R.B. No. 82, 1938.

WHYTE, WILLIAM FOOTE. *A Pattern for Industrial Peace.* New York, 1951.

INDEX